Guidance and Counselling

Guidance and Counselling

(Including Exceptional Children)

Preeti Singh

SHIPRA

Rs. 850

ISBN: 978-93-88691-16-1

First Published in India in 2019

Guidance and Counselling

Published by:

SHIPRA PUBLICATIONS
LG 18-19, Pankaj Central Marke,
I.P. Ext., Patparganj, Delhi 110092, India
Ph.: +91 11 22235152/6152, 9650028065
Email: info@shiprapublication.com
Website: www.shiprapublication.com

Preface

It is by the grace and blessings of the Almighty God that I am presenting a book on Guidance and counseling. This text is a response to the request made by my students and colleagues who are working in the field of Guidance and Counselling. It was they who motivated me through constant persuasion to undertake this venture. I hope the teacher educators, teachers and students will cherish my efforts.

The present book is an attempt to organize the subject content of Diploma in Guidance and Counselling, B.Ed and M.Ed courses of different universities. It covers key concepts related to each chapter in depth sequentially in simplest possible language. The present book is a humble effort to eradicate weaknesses which have been realized by both teacher educators and teacher trainees from time to time in subject guidance and counseling. It covers not only general but also specific aspects related to school guidance and counseling. It will be helpful not only for teacher educators dealing with this subject but also students of M.Ed, B.Ed, diploma, guidance workers, counselors, researchers, students of psychology and institutions working for social causes like NGOs. This text is an asset to those individual and organizations who are working for physical, mental, social and emotional health of students and striving hard for establishing new order for normal as well exceptional children.

At the very onset, the author is indebted to all eminent writers, thinkers, educationists and publishers whose work have been consulted and incorporated in the preparation of the book.

The author gratefully acknowledges the contribution of her family members, who have been pillars of strength in my work all through. The author is especially thankful to Shipra Publications who paved the way for the final outcome of the book.

27.03.2019 **Dr. Preeti Singh**

Contents

1

Guidance and Counselling

Meaning and Concept

Meaning and Concept of Guidance

The term *guidance* derives its meaning from the word 'Guide' which means to direct or to lead, the act of giving the needed information regarding place, problem, subject, situation, or individual. Giving information is an essential function of guidance. Guidance aims at helping an individual in recognizing, and utilizing his/her inner resources to set goals, make plans, and work out his own plan of development under most favourable conditions that society provides. According to Rishi Aurobindo Ghosh—"The first principle of true teaching is that nothing can be taught; the teacher is helper and guide; and he does not impart knowledge to his pupil but helps him to acquire knowledge for himself."

Guidance is a major field of education, but education on the whole is not guidance. Education is understood as guidance with a measure of imposition.

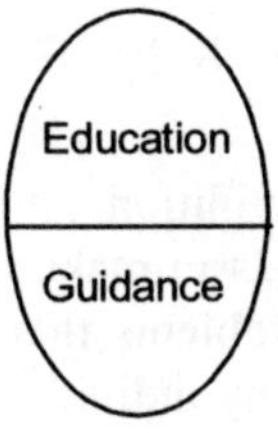

Guidance has been described by some experts as:

Arthur J. Jones

"Guidance is assistance given to individuals in making intelligent choices and adjustments."

John Dewey

"Teaching is guided self-guidance or guided self-development, which means that the purpose of education is to help individual to develop his inner potentials and abilities with the help of external environment like teachers, parents, and society."

Crow and Crow

"Guidance is assistance available by professionally qualified and adequately trained men and women to an individual or child to help him to:

1. Manage his life activities,
2. Develop his own point of view,
3. Make his own decisions, and
4. Carry out his own burden."

Shertzer and Stone

"(Guidance) is a process of helping individuals to understand themselves and their world... Guidance is means of helping individuals to understand and use wisely the educational, vocational and personal opportunities they have or can develop and guidance is a form of systematic assistance whereby students are aided in achieving satisfactorily adjustment to school and life."

Lefever

"Guidance is that systematic, organized phase of the educational process which helps the youth grow in his power to give point and direction to his own life to the end that he may gain rich personal experiences while making his own unique contribution to our democratic society."

To sum up the above definitions, it can be said that guidance is a process of helping individuals to make their own decisions. It merely gives an insight; solving problems that arise in life is primarily the individual's responsibility. Any individual, given skillful guidance, can develop capabilities like self-understanding, self-realization, self-orientation, self-direction, and self-decision making.

It is said that Guidance is putting round pegs into round holes—It means channelizing an individual's potentials in the right direction.

Counselling is one part of the large guidance programme in the education system, when the guidance programme is implemented in a school, it is termed as school guidance programme.

The Education Commission (1964-66) stressed that the guidance and counselling programmes assisting the students in choosing appropriate courses, and helping them in dealing with emotional and psychological problems, should be an integral part of the education facilities provided in institutions of higher education.

This Commission recommended that every school must have:

1. at least one counsellor for every one thousand students on roll in a school,
2. project for training professional counsellors should be organized in some university competent to do, and
3. the school must have Information and Employment Centres.

Assumptions behind Guidance Programme

1. It facilitates individuals in getting timely information.
2. Individuals have an innate urge to grow and develop—guidance helps them to use their potential in a better way.
3. It helps individuals to know about themselves better, for example self-understanding, self-dependent, self-realization, self-control, self-direction, etc.
4. It is only within the limits of genetic endowment or inherited capacities that individuals can grow, develop, and foster their own development.
5. Once an individual realizes its potential, environment plays an important role in development of individual's capacities to optimum.

Basic Concept of Guidance Programme

The fundamental concept of the guidance programme is the discovery of individual differences by psychologists. No two students are alike. They differ in heredity, in potential, in achievement, in interest, in aptitude, in need, and so on.

Principles of Guidance

The three principle of guidance are:

1. The worth and dignity of the student should be kept in mind at all costs.
2. It is not only the heredity, but also the environment which affects individual growth. Thus, the prime concern of guidance should be the optimum development of an individual within his environment.
3. An individual is a growing organism, having immense potential to grow and progress. With the help of proper guidance, an individual should be empowered to develop himself personally.

Principles of Guidance Services

1. *Guidance should be provided to all*: It should be extended to all students at every stage of education, especially in a democratic country like India. It should be equal regardless of their sex, locality, physical handicap, and intellectual capabilities, social and economic statuses.

2. *Guidance should continue throughout life*: Guidance is a continuous process of helping an individual to adjust himself to the environment, having at every stage an added capacity to grow. It is, therefore, felt that guidance should start from kindergarten stage, and continue right up to the level when the individual settles down in life completely. Guidance, being a lifelong process, is required even when an individual becomes very old.

3. *Guidance must be concerned with all areas of pupil's growth*: It must take into account the harmonious all-round development of the personality (educational, vocational, personal, social, etc.). Even in a vocation, guidance should not be limited just to the choice of vocation, but also include placement, adjustment, and research.

4. *Guidance requires co-operative efforts:* It should involve pupils, parents, teachers, principals, and the counsellor. A teacher who is also a true friend, philosopher, and a guide plays an important role in a student's life.

5. *Guidance is a major part of educative process:* Complete education is not confined to guidance alone. Guidance is a part of education, but not its sum. However, the two cannot be separated from each other.

6. *Guidance encourages self-discovery and self-discipline:* These are important aspects of ideal guidance. By directing individuals and interfering too much, we don't respect their independence, worth, and dignity; thereby we end up making them dependent on us. Minimum guidance gives individuals the choice of self-discovery and self-discipline.

7. *Guidance is beneficial for both individual and society:* In the process of guidance, there is a need to consider both the needs of the society and the individual.

8. *Guidance must consider individuals as average and normal:* It is wrong to think that guidance is needed only for those who are backward, and whose development has been retarded. It is meant for all.

Other than the above-mentioned given principles, it should be kept in mind that each individual has different abilities, capacities, interests, and aptitudes. The philosophy of guidance recognizes the importance of individual differences. It is also important that individual should be willing to avail guidance.

Purpose and Scope of Guidance

In Mathewson's view, the following are the purposes, and scope of guidance services:

1. ***Appraisal and Interpretation of Personal Characteristics***
   (a) *Self-understanding*—the discovery of aptitudes, capacities, and attributes of the self; weak and strong points.
   (b) Ability to evaluate the self in relation to personal and social experiences, and the more effective use of self in everyday living.

2. ***Adjustment to Schools, Teachers, and Pupils***
   (a) Satisfactory adjustment to academic work, getting the most out of studies, and school activities.
   (b) Diagnoses of severe learning problems, and their remedy.
   (c) Placement in suitable educational experience in accordance with individual needs and potentials.
   (d) Transfer from one course to another, from one programme to another, depending upon the need, performance and other circumstances.
   (e) Social adjustment of teachers and pupils.
   (f) Personal status in school—growth in self-confidence and acceptance of self.

3. ***Orientation according to Educational and Vocational Opportunities and Requirements***
   (a) Selection of appropriate courses in line with individual needs, interest, abilities, and circumstances.
   (b) Choosing various types of experiences from the complete school curriculum, including co-curricular activities.
   (c) Planning a total educational programme.
   (d) Choice of suitable and feasible type of advanced training programmes in colleges or other educational institutes in line with individual needs, and social requirements.
   (e) Selection and tentative broad areas of preparation for vocational pursuit.
   (f) Information on occupational opportunities and trends.
   (g) Aid in obtaining work experience.
   (h) Assistance in finding suitable employment.
   (i) Follow-up after school, help in early occupational adjustment.
   (j) Tentative choice of vocational activities in accordance with individual interest.

(k) Interpretation of school and democratic values, and relation of individuals to these values.

4. *Development of Personal Potentialities*

(a) Growth in intellectual, academic capacities, skill and understanding potential (personal).
(b) Development of favourable attitudes and habit dispositions.
(c) Understanding and assimilation of ideas and capacities to undertake consistent action in accordance with a social construct, and individually satisfactory life philosophy.

All school responsibilities are shared, to a greater or lesser degree, with home and community. All the guidance services and school programmes are basically concerned with activities promoting an all-round development of personality.

Need for Guidance Programme

Man is a social animal living in a society. He must resolve inner conflicts in order to cope with external demands. He needs to adjust with other human beings, and keep his mental balance while doing so. In the process of adjustment, he faces innumerable problems, and therefore, needs guidance. As a matter of fact, an individual needs guidance throughout his/her life. However, the stage at which guidance is needed most is when he/she is being educated and trained to take up a useful and productive role in society. This corresponds mostly to the period of schooling. It is in this period that potentialities are realized, abilities and skills developed, habits and attitudes formed, while social and emotional development takes place. A student, thus, needs guidance with respect to various aspects of life. The needs of guidance can be classified into two:

I. Individual needs
II. Social needs

I. Individual Needs

1. Academic growth
2. Vocational development
3. Personal and social development

1. *Academic Growth:* Every child is sent to school with the aim to develop his/her abilities and skills. If the teachers want to teach effectively, they must know well not only the subject which they teach, but also the children in their class. A guidance trainer tries to help the teachers in

understanding the children in the class about their needs, abilities, and interests to adjust their teaching accordingly, thus making it more successful. Knowing a particular child's ability and interest, the teacher can use appropriate teaching method in the development of his/her potentialities.

2. *Vocational Development:* Guidance is needed to develop positive attitude towards work. From the early school years, the students need to develop self-awareness and awareness about the world of work. This has become more complicated with the diversification of courses, and the new occupational opportunities which are fast developing. Besides self-awareness, the students need to develop their abilities, skills, attitudes, and interests in order to prepare themselves for the choice of suitable career.

If proper care is not taken to develop the required skills in children in their formative years of life; vocational guidance may not be of much help to them at a later stage.

3. *Personal-social Development:* A child faces many problems in his/her life. These problems may relate to his/her family, physical appearance, health, peer group, teacher, academic, and many other issues. The need for guidance in personal-social development has increased due to fast social changes. Children from the rural families migrating to cities, first generation learners, and children of working mothers need special attention to cope with varied problems.

Thus effective principles of guidance endeavour to improve interpersonal relationships.

II. Social Needs

1. Guidance for better family life.
2. Guidance for proper utilization of human resources.
3. Guidance for good citizenship and national development.

1. *Guidance for Better Family Life*

Better family relations and good social adjustment within the family are the basis of adjustment in the community. A lot must be done in the direction of improving good relationship between children and their family members. This will help in improving family life.

2. *Guidance for Proper Utilization of Human Resources*

- A job is important not only from the point of view of the individual who has to earn a living for himself, but also from the point of view of the society which builds up its resources from the output that each individual is able to bring forth.

- It is necessary that the individual who takes up a job is suited for it in terms of his abilities, skills, attitude, and personality traits.
- There is a need to derive satisfaction from the job done by an individual. It is only then that she/he can make a useful contribution to the society. For example, a teacher earns his/her living through teaching, and also improves literacy in society. A teacher, by his teaching, is deriving personal benefit as well as job satisfaction by contributing to the society.

3. *Guidance for Good Citizenship and National Development*

Guidance helps the school in inculcating in children an understanding of social values, needs, attitudes, habits, good manners, loyalties, and social responsibilities. It makes the students conscious of their rights and duties towards society. "Today's learner is tomorrow's leader."—Plato. Guidance helps individuals to be good citizens of the country and contribute to national development.

Identifying Learners' Needs

Guidance is need based. At the onset it is important to identify individual needs for which guidance is to be imparted. Needs can be divided as personal including social, educational and vocational. Once individual need is identified, a guidance plan can be prepared accordingly. For instance, if a person is looking for choice of subjects at +2 level, guidance needs to be given according to his academic achievements, aptitude, personality and the options available to him. Similarly, if he has problem in memorizing, the focus of guidance would be on his learning habits and home environment.

Essential Features of Guidance Programme

1. Orientation service
2. Individual inventory service
3. Educational and occupational information services
4. Counselling service
5. Placement service
6. Research and evaluation services

The school counsellor spends most of his/her time in helping students in planning their education and vocation. This is not an isolated or single activity, but a part of the complete guidance programme which touches the lives of all students. Guidance programme in a school involves many activities, and is a continuous process. A guidance counsellor is a trained person who functions systematically after carefully evolving a 'school guidance programme' by surveying the students' needs, and pooling in the physical and other resources of the school, after ensuring cooperation from the administrative authorities.

1. *Orientation of New Students*: Orientation programme conducted for new students plays an important role in their adjustment to that particular school. The counsellor, through the orientation activities, attempts to acquaint them with the diverse aspects of the school. They are informed about its history, traditions, purposes, rules and regulations, buildings, and physical facilities, faculty, students, curricular and co-curricular activities. This is also known as information service. These services are necessary while inducting young people into a school system. During orientation guidance worker also provides information about guidance services in schools and other related facilities around.

2. *Individual Inventory Service*: Information on various aspects of a student's personality and background needs to be collected in order to understand him and his needs; help him/her understand about his/her traits. The information to be collected includes home background, place of residence, education and occupations of the members of his/her family. Information is required about his/her abilities, interests, health, and general behaviour patterns. This information is collected from the student, and his/her parents to begin with, and thereafter from other sources. This may be through questionnaire and/or interviews.

A problem checklist may be administered to the student. Information is obtained from school records, including attendance, health, and achievement records. Observation of a student's behaviour also provides valuable information. The counsellor may also use psychological tests to get information about the student's aptitude and interests. The information thus collected is recorded on a Cumulative Record Card, which is readily available. The study of the card gives a comprehensive picture of the student. The individual inventory service involves exploratory experience and self-analysis.

3. *Educational and Occupational Information Services:* Collection and dissemination of educational and occupational information is essential for educational and vocational guidance. The counsellor provides information about different jobs, their nature of work, education, and

training required for entry, the training institutions, and the avenues of employment after training. Information about working conditions, income, and other monetary benefits is also imparted. The counsellor helps students in understanding the world of work. The counsellor collects information from a variety of sources: books, pamphlets, prospectuses of education and training institutions as well as advertisements give useful information. These are classified, and displayed in the occupational information service centre.

Useful charts are made depicting the occupations to which various courses will lead. These can show the education and training required, the methods of entry, salary, the avenues of promotions, and other benefits from various occupations. The counsellor may organize talks with representatives of various professions to give a firsthand account of the work, working conditions, and requirements of the job. Since new jobs are emerging, and occupational patterns are constantly changing; the counsellor has to continuously strive to keep the information up to date. Schools and colleges have to collect data about education and vocational opportunities for the benefit of their students. In some universities, student guidance bureau or information guidance bureau provides occupational information, and information regarding training facilities.

Anecdotal Records—Anecdotal records are a valuable source of information regarding the counselee. They are inexpensive tools, and do not require much training on the part of the recorder. The interpretation requires professional training. However, their main drawback is that they are subjective. If based on systematic and objective observations, anecdotal records can give valuable information about the social, emotional, and personal problems of the individual.

While using anecdotal records for purpose of counselling, one must allow some margin for exaggeration and distortion. The counsellor must also remember that they can make effective tools only when combined with data gathered through other means.

Cumulative Records—Evaluating cumulative records is a comparatively new development in education. They are often considered synonymous with the progress reports, which the school sends to the parents from time to time. The progress report is a record of attendance, examination marks, and the rank of the child in his class. Cumulative records, on the other hand, are more comprehensive than the records of attendance and achievement. They register the child's social adjustment in school, her/his behaviour with other children in the group as well as her/his attitude towards the teachers' estimate of the child's general adjustment, emotional maturity, and a number of other personality traits. A good cumulative record contains the counsellor's estimate of qualities like hard work, perseverance, tolerance, sociability, and such other attributes which make for a more complete picture of the child than the record of the attendance and examination marks.

The terms applied to all records which provide meaningful, significant, and comprehensive information about the individual over the years. As this information accumulates over a period, these records are called as cumulative records. In order to make practical use of these records, these records need to be maintained regularly, and made available to the counsellor as well as the teachers. Apart from this, teachers must also know how to interpret these records to the students, and their parents. This involves special training and skills for teachers, which they can develop through in-service training programmes.

These records help teachers and counsellors as they provide information regarding early history, family background, abilities, likes, dislikes as well as the student's special interests and aptitudes. These materials are often sufficient for the counsellor to plan interviews, with little need for exploration.

Records

S. No.	*Anecdotal*	*Cumulative*
1.	They have to be maintained regularly.	As the name suggests, they are collected things over a number of years. So, they are called cumulative records.
2.	They keep or provide information regarding social emotional problems.	They are synonymous to school progress report, but more comprehensive in nature.
3.	Useful for planning for interviews.	They give information regarding an individual.
4.	In-service training is required in order to avoid subjectivity.	Training is required to interpret the information to students and parents.
5.	Inexpensive.	Expensive.
6	It provides some tools to collect information.	It provides the personality traits of an individual.

4. *Counselling Services:* A counsellor helps students to understand themselves, and accept themselves as individuals. He/she also helps to develop in them greater ability to cope with, and solve their problems which increases their competence in making decisions and plans for the future.

The aim of vocational or education counselling services is to help the individual in making realistic choices. The counsellor helps the individual arrive at wise choices by considering his strengths, and weaknesses in relation to courses open to him. The individuals are enabled to weigh and evaluate their abilities, and limitations in relation to the opportunities, and draw up their requirements for an educational or vocational career so as to make realistic plans based on these considerations. Counselling services also help individuals in their social-personal adjustments and develop their personalities.

5. *Placement Services*: Placement usually indicates assistance in the form of training or study offered to students for jobs. The counsellor acts as a liaison officer between the student and the outside agency to secure jobs for his students. The counsellor also provides guidance on how to apply for a job, or gain entry into a training programme. The placement service is usually rendered by employment exchanges. The schools in India do not have any arrangements for vocational placement but they can help their pupils in education placement. The aim of placement services is to help the students in getting employment. It is the function of the school and colleges to provide placement services to its students. This is an essential part of guidance programme. There are many employment and information guidance bureaus doing commendable services for the placements of students community and also in many institutions of higher learning.

6. *Research and Evaluation Services:* Research is not a guidance service which is organized for the sake of the good of the individual. The aim of research services is to evaluate the techniques and methods used in the foregoing services, and check their effectiveness. They are undertaken with a view to making the entire guidance programme richer.

To find out whether the school guidance programme is according to the needs or the desired goals of its students, the counsellor functions as an evaluator or a researcher. The counsellor also works on improving the guidance programme. He/she designs a plan of action for the proposed work; identifies the problems, collects data and analyses the information received. The counsellor conducts occupational surveys and a great deal of research. The research may be based on the data collected through students' records. There can be various techniques to evaluate guidance services.

Methods of Evaluating Services: The methods of survey and experiment are adapted to help the students. In the experimental method, the behaviour of the group of students who have received guidance is compared with the other control group to whom guidance service is not offered, and the differences are studied and recorded. In the survey method, the status or position of guidance services in the school is surveyed.

Principles of Organizing Guidance Services

Guidance services in a school or college are to be organized keeping in focus its assumptions, principles and scope on one hand and needs of pupils on the other. A plan of action should be finalized in consultation of all stakeholders. In this sense guidance service is a facilitative service. It helps not only students but also teachers and parents in better understanding of the child. Principals and teachers can together plan these services.

The purpose of an organization in any field of work is the achievement of its objectives. The organisation endeavours to acquire that expertise on which its existence depends. In this sense, an organisational structure for the achievement of guidance purposes in education involves plan for relating the activities of guidance worker with one another, and with those of other members of the education team.

Nature of function determines the quantification of the workers. Experience in guidance determines the concepts, basic tools for the development of reasonably successful programmes.

1. *Guidance as Facilitative Service:* Guidance in education is a facilitative service for carrying out the objectives of education programme by providing facilities to the teacher, students, and the administrator for their development and success. The facilitative services make the most effective contribution to the work of teachers and administrators.

2. *Guidance Service for All Students:* Guidance is not meant only for those students who have some problem. It would be dangerous to identify guidance as a service for the deviant. It takes a holistic approach, bringing within its ambit all the students of the school. Thus, the effectiveness of guidance services is very largely dependent upon the importance accorded to it in a specific school.

3. *Guidance Service Involves various Stakeholders:* Not only the teaching staff, but also the administrative staff are equally important in

the functioning of the school guidance programme. The Administrator has the duty of planning curricular and co-curricular programmes aimed at meeting the common needs. A teacher plans and carries out programmes, keeping in view the needs and problems of each student. If a student is found to be lacking in studies, and is identified as an underachiever; it is the duty of the teacher to help him achieve the desired capacity of performance.

Besides the teachers, administrator, and guidance personnel, there are many others involved in guidance efforts. Apart from performance in studies, they also look into physical defects which affect the eye or ear, and provide appropriate guidance. School specialists of different departments like music, art, physical education, school psychologist, and school worker play their respective roles according to their specialized or professional competence in the educational process.

4. *Community Conditions Affect Organizations:* In the school guidance_programme, the services provided to children by their community is also considered. The community has youth, medical, and health centers. Under the school guidance programmes, these services of the community are utilized for the benefit of the students. The school can efficiently conduct its guidance programmes with the involvement of the community and the parents.

5. *Identification of a Leader:* The guidance programme needs a well-qualified and capable leader, who can command, and coordinate the programmes effectively.

6. *Adequate Provision for Implementation of Guidance Programmes:* The school must have qualified counsellors who can guide the students efficiently and effectively. In turn, the counsellors must be provided adequate time and facilities to work efficiently. Guidance must find its place in the school budget and the organizational structure. Space, equipment, and record of students must be well provided for.

7. *Adaptability of Guidance Programmes*: As the needs of students vary with time and space, the guidance programme should be so designed as to meet the changing needs of students. It means guidance programmes must be flexible. Different types of occupational and industry needs in the modern times have created different demands upon education and training facilities. The demand for management services having increased very rapidly in the recent years, also calls for a specialized education.

Issues and Problems of Guidance

Guidance programme in India is a recent development and is naturally confronted with various problems which may be classified as follows:

1. *Psychological Problems:* The programme of guidance is based on certain theories regarding the structure of human abilities. The techniques of guidance have to be evolved accordingly. There are extreme views, and confusing opinions on personality structure and its bearing on guidance. Psychologists believe in the General factor of intelligence. Recently there has been a shift in emphasis from intelligence to personality. The function of guidance is to orient an individual in the right direction.

Prof. Rama Rao has observed the following issues in guidance programme:

(i) Personality and success in vocations
(ii) Fundamental school skills and innate or constitutional capacities
(iii) Outcome of schooling and demand of occupations.

2. *Pedagogical Problems*: The next problem centers around the question of availability of norms. Without norms, it is not possible to have a coherent picture of either one's traits, or individual differences. The question of impact of heredity and environment on personality, intelligence etc.—though much discussed—is still open. The concept of culture free test is almost a dream, and thus every experimenter has to find the way out of the vicious circle after some amount of bewilderment and deliberations.

3. *Philosophical Problems:* Guidance is based upon the freedom of choice, and every theory of counselling implies an ethical position for those who view non-directive counselling as absolute freedom of choice of the ultimate goal of knowing themselves. There is no other absolute value towards which the counsellor may guide. But this knowledge of the self is too much to be expected from the school children.

4. *Sociological Problems:* The present society is undergoing rapid change. At this stage of transformation, from the existing pattern to a new pattern, various problems are arising. There is disharmony everywhere, and conflict at every stage. The socio-economic opportunities vary to a great extent. There is a striking disharmony between the courses provided, and the occupational opportunities.

The pressing demand for one course in preference to another gives rise to other problems of sociological nature. The choice of the majority for one or two courses is influenced by the prevailing sense of values attached to a particular course or career by society and the state. Dr. Rama Rao observed that it is difficult to relate schooling to employment, unless a school plans to match its manpower to the needs of major sectors of industry, agriculture, commerce, services, and other professions.

5. *Practical Problems:* Problems faced by the principals of schools are given below:

(a) Work out the guidance scheme, and encourage parents to view guidance as an aid in the present context.
(b) Translate the existing information in school into estimates of general ability.
(c) Start work where there is no accepted set of tools for guidance.
(d) Make provisions for transfer in case some of the students admitted for some practical courses do not find them sufficiently interesting.

The success of the scheme of guidance depends on how we meet these problems. It is found that most of the difficulties pertain to the organization, rather than psychology. It is, therefore, felt that there should be co-ordination among parents, employment exchange, teachers, headmasters and psychologists in order to formulate a practical scheme of guidance.

2
Spheres of Guidance
Educational, Vocational, and Personal-Social

EDUCATIONAL GUIDANCE

Educational guidance is aimed at helping students gain maximum benefit out of school education, and to solve their problems related to education at different levels.

Educational Guidance endeavours to focus on the following:

1. Give opportunities to students to discover, develop, and improve their interests and abilities.
2. Encourage students to develop good study habits.
3. Arrange for remedial work, when required.
4. Make students aware of the needs of educational planning.
5. Assist students in the right choice of their courses of study.
6. Give required information on higher education, and stimulate them to consider carefully.
7. Help the teachers and the principal in planning, and conducting the school education programme to promote maximum reach of education, and maximum development of students.

Educational Guidance is related to the following aspects:

1. Guidance and curriculum.
2. Guidance and classroom learning.
3. Guidance of special students—gifted, backward, underachievers, and dull.

Guidance and Curriculum

Relationship between education, guidance, and curriculum:

Education: It endeavours to prepare all youth for an effective participation in a society. It works on the development of pupils' social, emotional, moral, mental, aesthetic, and vocational competence. It prepares them for family living, civic, and community responsibilities.

Guidance: It brings about behavioural changes in pupils by training them to become more effective in solving their problems, and developing in them the ability of self-direction and self-understanding.

***Curricula*:** Appropriate courses need to be designed for promoting the students' growth, security, and accomplishment leading to effective living in society.

It is not true that the learner gains experiences only under the direction of teachers in the school. Besides classroom learning, the learner is exposed to guidance through administration, time management, extracurricular activities, home, and the community.

Rationale for Integration of Education, Guidance and Curriculum

1. *Similarity of Goals*

Goals of education, guidance and curriculum are similar, i.e. overall development of the child to develop as good citizen of the country. There is a shift in the curriculum, from subject-centered to student-centered. Therefore, the teacher has to focus on the student's competence and achievement. The teacher is expected to improve the quality and adequacy of instruction, and provide valuable learning experiences that will meet the needs of the students and help them solve their problems.

2. Similarity of Functions

1. Both guidance and curricula have the same function—to take complete care of the needs of the child.
2. Through guidance, efforts are made to identify the needs and interests of pupils.

Teachers need to interact with the same people—pupils, parents and the community and so the guidance worker.

3. *Similarity in Education Resource Materials*

Very often, the counsellors do not check to find out whether the guidance books kept in the library are being used or not. They, also, fail to check whether the teachers are aware about the availability of such books in the library. The guidance books help the teachers in preparing the curriculum, and education resource materials, in accordance with the specific needs of the students.

4. *Similarity in Methodology and Techniques of Working with Pupils*

There is need to explore ways and means of working with pupils to analyze how teachers, curriculum specialist, and guidance workers can work together to discover new means of resolving the problems of a specific group. In doing so, all would discover that more responsive ways of working with youth should be evolved to meet the needs of the child.

The counsellor and the teacher should work closely on the curriculum to be adopted according to the need or requirement of students. They work on new concepts for efficient management of the learners' needs.

5. *Similarity in Therapeutic, Preventive, and Developmental Approaches*

Through the close integration of guidance data and curricular experiences, both the teachers and guidance counsellors can deal with the problems of students, and in certain cases prevent them from arising in future. This way each student's guidance and learning will be purposeful, unified, and coordinated.

6. *Similarity of Problems*

Problems such as those of coordination, articulation, and communication have been of prime importance both in the field of guidance and teaching. Both have been concerned with transition from one situation to another.

Education Commission (1964-66) had suggested that the ultimate goal of education should be to introduce adequate guidance services in all secondary schools with a trained counsellor in charge of the programme.

Guidance needs to be made an organized service of the school, if it has to make its impact on the growth and development of a school child. If it is intended as an incidental activity of school, and is left to the good sense of every trainer, much of its significance will remain unexpressed.

Thus, in order to bring qualitative changes in today's educational process, it is essential to introduce this service in a well-organized way. It means systematic planning, coordination, and conduct of certain activities, wherein duties are allocated and responsibilities defined. All the concerned members work as a team with full understanding of each other's role and responsibility.

Guidance and Curriculum—Separate Activities

Guidance and Curriculum are separate activities and are different from each other. The differences can be observed as below:

1. *Differences in Terms of Specialization:* Teachers have the requisite specialization in, and the responsibility of teaching their particular subjects. They teach their subjects with different teaching methods. On the other hand, guidance personnel are required to counsel, keeping in

view the all-round development of the children. Both the teachers and the counsellors differ in their specialization and training.

This has fostered a feeling of insecurity in the teachers that they may be wrong about the diagnosis of a pupil's behaviour. They do not have the professional training like the guidance counsellor to identify the children's problems.

2. *Individual Approach Guidance vs. Curriculum Group Approach:* The democratic group functioning approach is being increasingly emphasized in all the new curriculum development, as a way of teaching and learning. Guidance and counselling follows both individual and group approach.

3. *Flexibility:* Curriculum framework is not at all flexible, and cannot be changed according to the different needs of students. The entire syllabus also needs to be finished within a stipulated time. On the other hand, guidance programme has flexibility, and is designed to solve different problems of students.

Curriculum designers have theoretical knowledge, and they are content oriented. Guidance viewpoints are not discussed therein. Under guidance, solution of practical problems requires humanistic and practical approach.

Guidance Based Curriculum

Guidance-based curriculum can be designed when teachers, curriculum staff, and guidance counsellors work cooperatively to create curricular experiences for pupils, who will also have a share in the process. A guidance based curriculum, therefore, requires the following:

1. Unity of purpose and function for strong team work.
2. Teachers should have a guidance perspective, knowledge of their pupil's needs, interests, and also recognition of their differences.
3. The teacher and counsellor must have knowledge of how children and young people learn. It is the teacher who understands students as individuals, and as group entities; which enables him/her to design a guidance based curriculum accordingly.
4. Guidance data can be a means of integrating guidance curriculum, provided that the guidance counsellors are able to perceive in what ways their data can be helpful to teachers in relation to designing a curriculum which will meet the needs of the pupils.

Teachers must realize in their efforts to integrate guidance and curriculum so that there is a content goal, and a guidance goal, and these goals function in an integrative manner. Each curriculum area, if properly interpreted, can also provide an opportunity for the development of better human relations, for analysis of personal aptitude, and for personal adjustment. Guidance based curriculum must be beneficial to pupils in terms of their goals, interests, and needs.

Role of the Teacher in Guidance and Counselling

Guidance and Classroom Learning

Guidance is a major part of education, but education as such is not guidance. Guidance during classroom learning proves beneficial in improving the teaching-learning situation as well as in solving problems encountered in a classroom.

Three Principles of True Teaching and Counselling

1. The first principle is that nothing can be taught. The teacher is a helper or guide, who does not impart knowledge to the pupil, but helps or facilitates them to acquire knowledge on their own.
2. The child learns according to her/his capacity and nature. Therefore, education should aim to draw out the best in a child.
3. The third principle of education is to work from the near to the far, from that which is, to that which shall be—education is an addition to the child's abilities, skills, and potentialities which are part of his/her heredity, surroundings, nationality, and country.

A free and natural growth is the condition of genuine development. Education is maximum development of all aspects of personality—physical, intellectual, moral, emotional, social, and spiritual. Harmonious development helps in exploiting all the innate potentialities of the human being and the individual becomes a worthy member of the society.

In teaching-learning situations, integration of guidance in classroom learning plays an important role in remedial guidance—A student failing in different subjects may take the help of the counsellor to understand whether the failure is a function of her/his own characteristics, the class, or some other cause. It is necessary for adjustment in classroom situation.

Guidance is a continuous process—There is need for continuous guidance when habits, attitudes, ideals are forming in children. Guidance develops the ability to choose the right occupational and social activities in adult life. It is preventive if the children begin to understand what they must avoid. As the saying goes, "Prevention is better than cure."

Guidance helps in solving problems related to learning—It helps in identifying reading difficulties, learning difficulties, late reading comprehension, likes and dislikes of students, difference in aptitudes and so on. Guidance aims to overcome these difficulties in students. Sometimes, a student may need prolonged guidance to overcome emotional barriers to learning.

Guidance helps in choosing the right course—Information regarding higher technical education related to work can be gained through the guidance programme. The counsellor can give appropriate guidance in advance about the suitability of a subject for the learner.

VOCATIONAL GUIDANCE

In the past, vocational guidance was the only help which was given by the guidance workers, which till date has remained an important service. Undoubtedly, the need for guidance for other subjects, apart from vocational, has gradually arisen. Vocational guidance assists the students in selecting the right occupation suited to them, and thereafter helps them in preparing for it, entering it, and progressing in it.

1. Vocational guidance has been defined as the process of assisting an individual in choosing an occupation, preparing for it, entering, and progressing in it.
2. Guidance is needed to develop a positive attitude towards work. From the early school years a student needs to develop self-awareness, and awareness about the world of work. This has become more complicated with the diversification of courses, and the new occupational opportunities that are developing fast. Besides self-awareness, a student needs to develop his/her abilities, skills, attitudes, and interests to prepare for the choice of a suitable career.
3. If proper care is not taken to develop the students during the formative years of their life, vocational guidance may not be of much help to them later.

A wise vocational choice requires the knowledge of one's physical characteristics, intellectual capacities, special aptitudes, and personality traits on the one hand, and the knowledge of various occupational groups, their requirements, and opportunities on the other. Vocational guidance should start early. Since vocational choices are related to the education process, it can be really effective if it is spread over the school years. The counsellor helps the students in educational and vocational planning through the following:

1. Helps the students to understand about themselves, their abilities, interests, values, and goals.
2. Provides information about occupations, nature of work, conditions of employment, opportunities for advancement as well as requirement for entrance, and success in the occupation as well as the abilities and skills required for it.
3. Gives information about various educational and vocational training institutions.
4. Evaluate strength and weaknesses of individual and match them with job requirement.

The counsellor helps the students to match information about themselves with the requirements of training institutions and jobs. He/she also motivates the students to think about their aims and aspirations and how to draw a plan of action. Vocational guidance is also referred to as career guidance.

Aspects of Vocational Guidance

1. Understanding of types and nature of work, various motives associated, place of work in one's life.
2. Understanding career development.
3. Know approaches to career development—Roe's trait factor theory, Holland's theory of early determinate vocational choice, and Super's theory of self-concept.

Activities of Vocational/Career Guidance

- Organization of career class/seminars
- Organization of career exhibition
- Establishment of career library
- Bringing out career publication
- Field Activities for collection of information and identify resources.
- Organizing Job Fest for placements.

Nature of Work

1. It is designed to operate a change.
2. It is required for the need of civilization.

3. It has some utility.
4. It helps imperfect to become perfect.
5. It satisfies basic needs and desires of people.

Terms Related to Work

1. *Occupation*—A group of similar jobs in several establishments; like teaching and counselling.
2. *Job*—A group of similar positions in one particular factory or organization: teachers, managers, principals.
3. *Work activity*—the content of a particular job.
4. *Work situation*—it is the context and environment in which one is working.

Why do People Work?

One of the main aims to work is to get a job, and earn money for living. A research study has shown that out of every 100 individuals, there are 80 per cent people who need to work to establish their identity.

Super says that work is needed to satisfy human aspirational needs. It provides opportunity for self-expression to keep life interesting. Work and way of life are related as work decides the class to which an individual belongs.

Classes in society are based on the income earned through specified work, which defines the social status of persons in society.

Education also determines job status, and leads to social mobility. A person from lower middle class may move upwards; e.g., the offspring of a middle class farmer becoming an IAS officer.

Occupation ensures class feelings and belongingness. It gives a feeling of solidarity. It is a kind of group dynamics. A group of teachers favours' other teachers. Similarly, engineers have their contacts with people in similar jobs. Teachers feel that they belong to teaching community.

Work changes the values and attitudes of a person towards a particular job. For example, if an introvert person becomes a teacher, she/he slowly learns to talk, and participate in social gatherings because it is a requirement of the job.

Physical conditions of work affect the person's attitude. For example, there is difference in the working conditions of a police officer at the police station from that of a teacher in school. Some jobs require order and discipline. In fact, every occupation demands a different kind of social behaviour.

Work impacts the routine and lifestyle. For example, a woman working as a teacher has the dual responsibility of managing household work, and teaching in the school or college.

Types of Work

1. Laymen's Classification:
   White collar jobs—mental work
   Blue collar jobs—manual work
2. Holland, a psychologist, classifies work in six categories:
   (a) *Realistic*—attracted towards technical and skilled jobs
   (b) *Intellectual*—scientists
   (c) *Social*—teachers, lawyers, social workers
   (d) *Conventional*—clerical, computer operator
   (e) *Enterprising*—private, sales people
   (f) *Artistic*—painter, musician, actor.
3. Anne Roe, another psychologist, categorizes work as:
   (i) *Service*—government jobs, administration etc.
   (ii) *Business*—depending on businessman's interest
   (iii) *Organization*—human relations
   (iv) *Technology*—engineers
   (v) Outdoor
   (vi) Science
   (vii) General cultural
   (viii) Arts and entertainment
4. Classification by Advert
   (a) *Professional*—CAs, engineers
   (b) *Prospectors*—managers
   (c) *Clerical*—clerks
   (d) *Skilled*—mechanics
   (e) *Semi-skilled*—drivers
   (f) *Unskilled*—domestic helpers

Vocational Development

Vocational life stages given by Buchler follow the general pattern of development:

1. *Growth*—significant from 0-14 years.
2. *Exploration*—15-24 years. It is an age when an individual begins to discriminate between imagination and reality, and becomes realistic.

3. *Establishment*—25-44 years, when a person progresses into a stable position. Working somewhere, following a profession, or a talent, or engaged in business, etc.
4. *Maintenance*—one tries to maintain one's achievements from 45-60 years.
5. *Retirement*—Even after official retirement, some people keep themselves busy, like writing books or following a hobby.

Factors Influencing Vocational Development

Vocational Choice

Ginsberg suggested three basic elements.

1. Occupational choice is a developmental process; it is not a single decision made at a point in time. It is a process which takes place over a period of 6 to 10 years.
2. Since each decision during adolescence is related to one's experience up to that point, and in turn has an influence on future, the process of decision making is basically irreversible.
3. Since occupational choice involves the balancing of a series of subjective elements with opportunities, and limitations of reality, the crystallization of occupational choice inevitably has the quality of a compromise.

Factors Influencing Occupational Choice and Vocational Development

In Allport's view, personality is a dynamic organization within the individual of those psycho-physical systems which determine one's unique adjustment to his/her environment. It is a product of both heredity and environment. The nature of the career patterns is determined by the individual's parental socio-economic level, mental ability, personality characteristics, and opportunities to which she/he is exposed.

Role of the Family in Career Choices

The abilities, interests, physique, and personality of an individual, which play such an important role in vocational development, are partly determined by heredity factors (parents and ancestors).

Physical factors, such as the geographical location of the home, physical conditions prevailing in the home, etc. have an effect on vocational development of the individuals.

Other physical conditions such as overcrowded house, lack of proper light and ventilation, and an inadequate diet etc. may have an impact on the health, thereby affecting the ability to study, which may lead to poor vocational development.

The socio-economic level of the family appears to exercise the most potent influence of all. The occupational information which the individual picks from his/her family will influence his/her vocational thinking and choice of occupation.

The family as a mediator of culture also influences vocational development, through caste values and opportunities, and religion, which is mediated through family, etc.

The family religion can at times gives a biased opinion about the choice of occupation. The family instills attitudes and values. Emotional currents in the family also have a subtle influence on vocational development. The family provides the earliest adult role models with whom the individual may identify or reject. For example, a boy wants to be like his father, and therefore, incorporates within himself his characteristics, including his occupational role, work values, and attitudes.

Other Factors Affecting Career Choices

Ability: Individuals with high IQ tend to seek and prepare for jobs which require highest level of intelligence and vice versa.

Personality: An individual's personality affects his/her vocational interests. For instance, good teachers are usually social, communicative, self-confident, and self-sufficient.

Merely work skills and abilities are not the sole determinants of success of an individual in a particular job. Good personal adjustment and interpersonal communication skills are also necessary.

Economic factors: While planning a career, an individual avoids those jobs which carry low wages and low prestige. This is because people are attracted towards jobs which offer high wages and high prestige.

Public policy: Policies like reservation—both in admission and jobs—makes it possible for people belonging to SC/ST to opt for some vocations, even with less experience and qualification.

Sometimes, high caste individuals are not able to choose streams like medicine or engineering even with good marks, because there is no reservation for them. Thus, they need to change their vocation despite aptitude and ability.

Theories of Career Development

The process of assisting an individual to choose an occupation by preparing for it, entering, and progressing in it has a wide scope. Vocational guidance and vocational education are interrelated subjects.

Vocational guidance solves problems concerning selection of a vocation, and provides solutions to problems.

The process of vocational guidance deals with interests, abilities, and emotional state of the mind of an individual while evaluating the chances of his/her success in a job. Apart from this, strengths and weaknesses are evaluated and then they are matched with job requirements. Theories of Career Development are:

- Parson's Trait and Factor Theory (1909)
- Roe's Personality Development Theory (1956)
- Holland's Personality Theory (1966), (1973), (1985)
- Super's Theory of Career Development (1990)

Trait and Factor Theory

Frank Parson in his book *choosing a Vocation* developed the approach of Trait and Factor Theory. He said that an individual's choice of a vocation depends upon:

(a) Clear understanding of the limits and strength about the person's mental traits, interests, intelligence and aptitude.
(b) Perfect knowledge of the needs, requirements, uses and abuses, in order to progress in different vocations.
(c) One of the theories of the trait and factor is adjustment between **A** and **B** regarding vocational development.

Differential psychology is concerned with the examination of individual differences in terms of traits and factors.

Hypothesis

1. Hereditary characteristics do not indicate specific vocational choice.
2. Pattern of development of abilities depends on the direction in which psychic energy is expanded voluntarily.
3. Direction of psychic energy depends on early childhood satisfaction and frustration.

Personality Development Theory

Roe's emphasis on early childhood experiences and Holland's typology of a person laid the foundations of the personality theory.

Anne Roe was a clinical psychologist, who stated that a person's vocational choice depends on the structure of childhood experiences. This experience relates to the child's needs and wishes—when satisfied in the childhood, he/she is motivated to choose some vocation which helped fulfill them. This theory indicates that every individual inherits a tendency to expand energies in some particular way. The innate tendency of expanding psychic energy combined with various childhood experiences moulds the general style of an individual to satisfy needs. The resulting style has specific and major implications for career behaviour or vocational choices.

Hypothesis on Relation of Early Experiences to Vocational Choice

1. The heredity basis for intelligence, special abilities, interests, attitudes, and other personality variables seem usually to be non-specific.
2. The pattern of development of special abilities is primarily determined by the direction in which psychic energy comes to be experienced involuntarily.
3. These directions are determined, in the first place, in the patterning of early satisfactions and frustrations.
4. The direction of psychic energy is the major determinant of the field to which person will apply himself/herself.
5. Needs satisfy themselves. They do not develop into unconscious motivators.
6. The satisfaction of needs, even if delayed but eventually accomplished, will become unconscious motivator, depending on the degree of satisfaction felt.

Maslow's hierarchical classification of needs has an implication on vocational development. He states that higher needs cannot appear until lower order needs are, at least, relatively well satisfied.

Basic Needs

1. Physiological needs
2. Safety needs
3. Belongingness and love
4. Need for self-esteem
5. Need for self-actualization

Patterns of Early Childhood Experiences with Parents or Family Atmosphere

The specific behaviours' of parents are of less importance than their attitudes towards the child. The major sub-division refers to the child's position in the family.

1. Emotional concentration on the child leads him/her to experience over-protection, and he/she becomes over-demanding.
2. Avoidance of the child develops negative attitude. Emotional rejection of a child, lack of gratification is intentional; neglect of the child is rarely intentional or voluntary.
3. Acceptance of the child.

Reflection of Early Experience in Vocational Choices

Persons growing up in child-centered families, who do not develop primary self-concentration, will be quite constantly aware of the opinions and attitudes of other persons towards themselves, and of the need to maintain self-position in relation to others.

Persons brought up in rejecting homes may develop intense defensive awareness of others. They may strongly reject persons, and react defensively towards others.

Those from accepting homes may have interest in other people. They will not be defensive, nor carry the sort of uncertainty that many in the first group show.

Implication of this Theory for Counselling

1. Vocational choice is closely related to personality characteristics developed during early childhood.
2. Vocational counselling is logical as it aims at helping the individual effectively in understanding needs, and abilities to identify occupations in which those needs can best be satisfied in consonance with abilities.
3. In this, activities are oriented towards identifying a student's psychological needs structure to match the resulting hierarchy of needs with those offered by various occupations.

In this way, it is helpful to students by:

1. Evaluating the potential of various fields for the satisfaction of current needs.
2. Further evolving a hierarchy through interview procedure. The emphasis on occupational information is designed to enable the student make the most expeditious use of his/her abilities.

John Holland's Theory Based on Personality Traits

Based on typology of personality, Holland's assumptions underlying his theory are:

1. "In our culture, most people can be categorized as one of the six types—realistic, investigative, artistic, social, enterprising, or conventional."
2. "There are six types of environment—realistic, investigative, artistic, social, enterprising, or conventional."
3. "People create an environment particular of their type."
   "People search for [the kind of] environment that will let them exercise their skills and abilities, expressions, their attitudes and values, and take on agreeable problems and roles."
4. "A person's personality is determined by an interaction between his heredity and environments."

In addition, Holland refers to some other key concepts as under:

1. *Consistency*—some personality types have more in common with other types. *It also d*emonstrate the relationship between the different types.
2. *Differentiation*—some people and some environments are much closer to one type; whilst other people and environments are much more a mixture of types.
3. *Congruence*—there are degrees of fitness between people and environments, e.g. a realistic type fits best into a realistic environment, and next best into investigative.

Some other concepts are as follows:

1. *Realistic*: Physically strong, unsociable, aggressive, lacks verbal skills, but has good motor coordination, e.g. car mechanics, radio operators, plumbers, surveyors.
2. *Investigative*: Needs to understand, likes thinking through problems, task oriented, has conventional values and attitudes, e.g. geologists, design engineers.
3. *Social*: Sociable, responsible, and religious. Has verbal and interpersonal skills, prefers to solve problem through feelings, e.g. counsellors, social workers, speech therapists, teachers, etc.
4. *Conventional*: Conforming to social norms. Likes well-structured tasks, values, material possessions, and status. Prefers numerical activities and subordinate roles, e.g. bank clerks, quality counsellors.

5. *Enterprising*: Uses verbal skills for selling, leading. Likes ambiguous social tasks, has greater concern for power and status, e.g. T.V. producers, hotel managers, etc.
6. *Artistic*: Tends to be introverted. Rejects conventional values, but has high ideals. Has a need for individualistic expression, gross physical skills, e.g. authors, composers, stage directors, commercial artists.

Holland states that a person's primary direction of choice is determined by the model type he resembles, e.g. investigators, scientists.

He perceived that the realistic and investigative types as more stable in their choices, and felt that the entrepreneur, social, and artistic types have high aspirations. He also associated high educational aspirations with investigative, social, and artistic characteristics as opposed to realistic types. Creativity is most associated with investigative and artistic.

Working environments are largely created by the typical characteristics of those working within them. Holland, like Roe, emphasized early childhood developmental experiences.

Weaknesses: Weinrach (1979) lists numerous weaknesses:

1. Holland's model is sexist, although he does admit to a lack of data on women.
2. This theory does not explain how people became the realistic investigator social, conventional, enterprising and artistic as categorized by it.
3. He has emphasized the value of the self-directed search. He underplays or opposes the need for individual help and counselling.
4. It provides a matching process which is described as static and simplistic.

Why many Consider Holland's Theory the Best

1. It was the latest and broadest theory which took into account the weakness of other theories.
2. He considered intelligence and personality a result of both heredity and environment.
3. Self-concept is regarded as a positive lead to higher vocation.
4. This theory can be tested very easily by creating lists like TAT, Rorschach to discover individual orientations.

Super's Theory of Self-concept

Developmental Approach

Donald Super has worked on occupational choice theory. His works, spread extensively over a long period of time, are based upon research on both sides of the Atlantic.

He has stated a few propositions:

1. Individual differences: People differ in their abilities, interests, and personalities.
2. Every individual has multi-potential; like Kapil Dev is not only cricketer, but is also a businessman. So a person could be a scientist and a musician.
3. Due to differences in ability pattern, some people are qualified for different occupations.
4. Although self-concept is generally fairly stable from late adolescence till maturity, making choices and adjustments are a continuous process throughout life.
   The process may be summed up in a series of life stages characterized by growth, exploration, establishment, maintenance, and decline.
5. The career pattern is determined by the individual's parental socio-economic level, mental ability, personality characteristics, and by the opportunities to which he/she is exposed.
6. Development through the life stages can be guided partly by facilitating the maturation of abilities and interest; and partly by developing self-concept.
7. Process of vocational development leads to developed self-concept.
8. Guidance workers help in attaining adjustment by compromising between self-concept and realities.
9. Work satisfaction and life satisfaction depend upon adequate outlets for an individual's abilities, interests, personality traits, and values.
10. The degree of satisfaction any individual attains depends on the degree to which he/she can implement self-concept.
11. Work and occupation help in organizing and defining personality. Although, for some people this focus is peripheral, incidental, or even non-existent.

Super's developmental approach is focused on five life stages, and these are described below:

1. Growth (birth to fourteen years)
   (a) Fantasy (0-4)—needs or demands dominate
   (b) Interest (11-12)—diverse activities seem attractive
   (c) Capacity (13-14)—abilities are considered in conjunction with job requirement
2. Exploration stage (15-24 years)
   (a) Tentative (15-17)—tentative choices are made and tried out in fantasy, discussions, and work.
   (b) Transition (18-21)—reality factors are given more attention as the individual enters work, training, etc.
   (c) Trial (21-24)—a suitable choice is tried out.
3. Establishment stage (24-44 years)
   (a) Trial (24-30)—a job or jobs are likely to be tested for suitability.
   (b) Stabilization (31-44)—a pattern emerges, and the individual attempts to secure his/her position at work.
4. Maintenance (44-64)—work position is consolidated.
5. Decline (65+)—retirement or reduction in work role.

More recently in 1981, Super used the concept of role to illustrate the variety of ways in which the individual conducts his life over a lifetime. In his life career rainbow, there are nine potential roles which can be occupied at some stage. They are parent, homemaker, spouse, worker, citizen, student, child, and pensioner.

These roles are conducted within four principal theatres—home, community, education, and work. There may arise conflict in two roles, such as in work role and parent role. A mother finds it difficult to manage household chores during office hours.

Osipow (1973) regards Super's theory as a 'well-ordered', highly systematic representation of the processes of vocational motivation; although he felt that he had given insufficient attention to social and economic factors that influence career decisions.

Super's work has stimulated the practice of carrying out career programmes in British schools. He laid the theoretical basis for career education.

However, Kline (1975) contends that Super's theory does not justify the name, because it does not give any new insight into vocational guidance. While summarizing different theories, he says:

> "As [a] conceptual model, Super's theory seems to be [the] most highly developed and advanced. This is reflected in its

explicitness, its fairly high degree of empirical support, and its substantiality in the large number of applications to human affairs. The personality style approach, on the other hand, seems to be the most amenable to the experimental and scientific method, and the closest to basic psychological concepts, but still lacking in a wide base of empirical support."

Occupational Information

The occupational information:

1. Makes guidance informative,
2. Enables the students to take own decisions by interpreting suitability of their decisions,
3. Helps in educational and vocational planning, and
4. Helps in revising old courses and develop new ones.

In this sense, Guidance service is informative, motivational exploratory, evaluative, and adjusting, and thus proving helpful for students.

Meaning of Occupational Information

- It includes facts on the nature of work
- Occupational relationships
- Working conditions
- Educational requirements
- Employment opportunities

Types of Information

1. *Information*—The information regarding different occupations can be provided through various Newspapers, Gazettes, UPSC, NCERT, YMCA.
2. *On the job training*—This kind of information can also be provided through Advertisements in newspaper, Magazines, Advisors of industrial establishment.
3. *Trends, patterns and growth of educational training opportunities*—census report 1991, 2001, 2011 year book, scheme of self empowerment and career clubs.
4. *Scholarships/fellowships*—Different types of schemes and the availability of fellowships and scholarships by CSIR, UGC, Ministries, international organizations and community trusts, assistance from banks, YMCA, Rotary clubs.

5. *Educational training facilities*—Prospectus of universities, Directories of training institutions, Handbook of training Facilities, Advertisements, etc. The need and background of students decide the type and amount of information required to be collected. Collection of information is a continuous process and it is necessary to make it up to date.

Methods of Collecting Information

Survey—It could be of different types.

1. *Wants ads survey*—cheapest and easiest method of collecting information. It provides current information.

2. *Alumni follow up survey*—old students are contacted, information is collected about occupation in which they are engaged.

3. *Community survey*—in this the different employing agencies are contacted personally. It provides latest information regarding requirements and trends.

It is not enough to collect information. It should be put in a usable form. This requires technical aspects and association with institutions and their libraries responsible for keeping such records.

Steps

1. Procurement
2. Study
3. Storage
4. Referring, indexing
5. Display and dissemination

Occupational Classification and Industrial Classification

Occupational Classification—it includes what an individual does. It is a type of work performed by an individual, irrespective of the branch of economic activity to which he is attached, e.g. a carpenter may work in ship building industry or steel plant, but by occupation he will be a carpenter.

Industrial Classification—it shows the position of an individual (worker) in the economic structure of an industry. His industry is type of service/good employer produces.

Method of Disseminating Information

1. *Group Method:* It is more suitable and its advantages are as under.

- Orientation can be given to all students.

- More economic, saves time.
- Experiences of several individuals can be pooled for the benefit of each member of the group.
- Those in need of individual counselling can be identified.

2. *Individual Method*: Its merits and demerits are as under,

- Best for dissemination of occupational information.
- Only for those who can't be helped through groups.
- It is difficult to organize.
- Expensive, time consuming.

Group Techniques of Imparting Occupational Information

- Through subject teachers by visiting places
- Career education (work sample project)
- Career discussions (films and film strips)
- Dramatization (special card catalogue)
- Career conference (career exhibition)
- Tutorials (through library)
- Bulletin board.

PERSONAL-SOCIAL GUIDANCE

The term 'personal-social' means those aspects of a student's life which relate to self and society. Every student faces certain problems about which he/she may be very anxious. Generally, they try to cope with the problems on their own. They may make mistakes, thus making the problem worse. The guidance programme aims at helping the students understand, and solve their problems through individual and group guidance. They may be made to realize that some of the problems faced by them are normal, and are faced by other students as well during this period. However, some problems may be more serious which require special attention. Students' problems may relate to:

1. Social adjustment
2. Family relations
3. Self-concept and personality
4. Adolescent health worries
5. Spending leisure time

(1) Social Adjustment—Friendship, getting along with other adolescents, and accepting them is an indicator of normal development. Friendship is important for an adolescent's emotional growth. Sometimes,

elders do not approve of students having friends. Some students may find it difficult to get along with others, and accept them the way they are. In such situations, the students need guidance to develop satisfactory interpersonal relationship. This guidance is given by a trained counsellor, who is neither a parent nor a teacher, but understands the emotional needs of adolescents. Guidance is needed to help them understand that individual differences are normal. Students of different castes and communities get along well with each other. Students must also appreciate the fact that others may have their own problems. This will help them to tolerate others' behaviours which they may not understand. Acceptance of self and others will minimize jealousy and aggression, and will help students to learn, to be considerate, kind, and cooperative.

(2) Family Relationships—The family plays an important role in the life of individuals. It gives them emotional and moral support. Sometimes, lack of proper understanding gives rise to conflicts between parents and children, or between siblings. Adolescents need to know that their problems are normal, and that nearly all young people experience them. However, occasionally there are real difficulties, and the counsellor may have to work with parents to help them understand the child's point of view. Sometimes, difficulties arise for students due to family conflicts or broken homes. In such cases, the counsellor may provide emotional support to such students, and help them to develop a healthy and workable relationship with their parents and other family members.

(3) Self-Concept and Personality—Development of an adequate self-concept is important for every individual. Young people are unsure of themselves. They do not know their own potential. Critical remarks, or even casual comments, can make them feel inferior or insecure. Acceptance by others is important for the development of healthy self-concept. Further, they should have the opportunity to learn about their own abilities, and to know and accept their strong and weak points. It is the responsibility of the counsellor to help the students understand themselves.

(4) Adolescent's Health Worries—Adolescents are often concerned about their own physique at this stage. They become self-conscious due to the rapid physical changes, such as sudden gain in height, weight, strength, and changes due to puberty. These make them conscious and anxious making many adolescents suffer from irritability, laziness, depression, and moodiness. They need guidance to develop healthy attitude towards physical transformations which lead to adulthood.

(5) Spending Leisure Time—The school students participate in many co-curricular activities like games and sports, debates, and dramatics, scouting and NCC, etc. Through participation in various activities, students find outlets for expression of their abilities and emotions. Many students, however, need opportunities for self-expression through art and craft. Some students are shy, and need encouragement. Guidance helps these students to find opportunities for utilization of their leisure time creatively, and development of their talents.

3

Counselling

The Heart of Guidance Programme

Literally, the term counselling derives its meaning from the word counsel which means to give advice, consultation, opinion, or suggestion. An individual seeks advice in a variety of situations and problems. For example, educational, occupational, personal, marital, medical, etc., advice or suggestions are given by parents, friends, teachers, and well-wishers.

However, guidance workers do not consider counselling as giving advice by the counsellor to the counsellee. It is also not giving solutions to the problem, or giving information or answers to questions. It is a relationship between the individual who needs help (counsellee) and a trained person (counsellor) who can provide help. It is aimed at helping the counsellee to gain understanding, and find his/her own direction. The counsellor helps him/her during the process of counselling to enhance his/her personal development, and to facilitate his/her social development by developing necessary social skills to meet the challenges of modern life.

Definitions of Counselling

E.G. Vedanayagam

> "Counselling is an accepting, trusting and safe relationship in which clients (or the counsellees) learn to discuss freely what upsets them, to define their goals, to acquire the essential social skills, and to develop the courage and self confidence to implement desired new behaviour."

Carl Rogers

> "A definitely structured permissive relationship which allows the client to gain an understanding about himself to a degree which enables him to take positive steps in the light of his new orientation."

Erickson

"A counselling interview is a person to person relationship in which one individual with some problem and needs turns to another person for assistance."

Webster's Dictionary

"Counselling is consultation, mutual interchange of opinion, or deliberating together."

H.B. Mc Daniel

"Counselling is a series of direct contacts with the individual aimed at offering assistance in adjusting most effectively with himself and his environment."

To summarize the above definitions counselling is a harmonious and trusted relationship between counsellor and counsellee where counsellor helps client in gaining insight into the solution of a problem.

Counselling—The Central Activity of Guidance Service

Counselling is an integral part of guidance programme. It is the heart of the guidance programme. The information service, the self-inventory service, the personal data collection service that precede it, lead up to it. The remaining services, for example, the preparation, the placement, follow up, and research services, etc. stem from it.

Counselling is that part of the guidance process in which the counsellor assists the counsellee to select his area of interest, or to solve the problem that confronts him. The problem is not solved by counsellor for the counsellee. He simply helps in thinking through the problem himself and in developing plans and attitudes needed for solving it. Though it may be considered a small part of total guidance programme, it is very significant. Most of the activities of the guidance programme are planned and carried out for the primary purpose of complementing the counselling service, because the process of choosing personal goals is essentially an individual undertaking in which counselling must occupy the control of the gathering and recording of data about the individual pupil, the collection, catalogueing, and filling of information about occupation training opportunities and other resources in the school, and in the neighborhood, representing only a few of the activities that make counselling an effective core of the guidance programme.

Counselling is distinguishable from other guidance activities because of certain special features that it possesses which makes it the focal point of the guidance programme. These features are:

1. It is a purposeful activity—a purposeful learning experience for both the counsellor and the counselle.
2. It is a private interview between the counsellor and counsellee when it is not a group counselling.
3. It is one to one relationship based upon the mutual confidence of the two parties concerned, and which grows out of the counsellee's recognition of assistance, and the presence of an adult person who is prepared to provide the assistance. Counselling as guidance service assists each individual student to make more effective adjustment to the environment in which he lives.

Characteristics of the Counselling Process

It is a process of mental understanding with the counsellor assisting the counselee to achieve optimum development.

1. *The counselling process is a joint quest*: It is carried out by counsellor and counsellee both. The counsellor's responsibility is to assist the individual in the process whenever he needs his help. The counsellor gives new insight, but does not dominate. He listens more than he talks, he helps the individual to understand himself, and opens opportunities for his best development.

2. *Counselling is a structured relationship*: One person turns to another for solution of problems. The counsellor helps the client by giving insights, suggestions, and advice if they are demanded, and accepted by the counsellee.

Steps to be taken in the counselling process:

(i) Establishment of relationship through rapport formation.
(ii) New orientation through insight.
(iii) A change in attitude that the client can solve the present problem himself, and will be able to solve such problems in future when they arise. The actual process of counselling involves interviewing after establishing rapport.

3. *Counselling is an individual matter*: The individual students who need help constitute the counselling process. The counsellor simply sets

the stage and the entire drama is played by the counsellee himself when it is non-directive or client centered approach of counselling.

4. *Counselling is continuous process*: Neither does it begins when the counsellee comes for help, nor does it ends when the counselee leaves satisfied.

5. *Counselling is a complex process*: The counsellor must study the problem faced by the client in detail. The solutions to the different problems are varied, and some of them are very complex. The counsellor has faith in the individual's ability to help himself, to understand himself, to find himself what has failed him, to gain insight into the ways of facing problems and solving them. He offers insight into the problem by repeating significant parts of the client's conversations, or by a question that helps him to explore the solution.

6. *Counselling is an eclectic process*: There is no single method of solving a problem; hence other methods are also adopted.

Purpose or Scope of Counselling

According to A.N. Boy and G.J. Pave, following are the important purposes of counselling:

1. To help the counsellee feel better, i.e. to help the counsellee accept himself.
2. To diminish the disparity between the real self and the ideal self; and to help persons think more clearly in solving their own personal problems.
3. To help students become more mature, and more self-activated.
4. To help students move forward in a positive and constructive way.
5. To help students to grow, and socialize by utilizing their own resources.

Counselling Skills and Characteristics of Good Counsellor

A school counsellor has a special position in the school. He is a professional, who is concerned with the development of each student. In order to carry out his/her responsibility effectively, he/she should have the following characteristics:

1. *Acceptance*—The counsellor must accept each student as a person of worth. Through action, words, gestures, or facial expression, the counsellor must be able to communicate his/her acceptance to the student.

Acceptance is not necessary only in counselling, but it is basic in all guidance situations.

2. *Trust*—Counselling success is based on mutual trust. The student may not confide in the counsellor unless he trusts the counsellor. The student needs the assurance that the counsellor will not disclose any information related to him, to the principal, teachers, parents, peers, etc. The counsellor must explain the principle of confidentiality. If the counsellor feels the need to talk about a student's problem to any other significant person, he/she should get the student's permission to do so.

3. *Listening with understanding*—The counsellor should be a sympathetic listener. He must listen attentively, and try to understand the feelings behind the student's line of thinking.

4. *Effective communication*—Passive listening can become tiring and uninteresting but listening is very important in counselling. However, if the counsellor is able to talk to the student, he/she will be able to draw valuable information for understanding the problems and their causes. Effective communication is the key to proper understanding of the students.

5. *Mutual respect and cooperation*—The counsellor must respect the students, and understand their behaviour. The counsellor must create the right environment, so that the students can respect him/her. They should try to remember the name of the particular student coming for guidance for the first time, along with other important details. The entire process of counselling is based on mutual respect. A good counsellor is also able to motivate the students to be cooperative with him/her, and enable them to participate in the counselling process.

6. *Empathy*—This means that the counsellors should be receptive enough to understand the problems of the students from their point of view. The counsellor should be able to communicate this empathy to the students with warmth and sincerity. Only then will the students realize that the counsellor is with them to share their problems. Counsellor should not be judgmental.

7. *Honesty*—A counsellor must be honest with the students. Along with guiding them, the counsellor should accept the strengths and weaknesses of the students. It is only then that the counsellor can make the students aware about their true potential; what they are capable of doing, and what they are not. However, the counsellor needs to do this tactfully, and gently, so that the students in question do not get hurt or feel inferior.

8. *Ability to recognize and encourage good points*—Every individual

is endowed with some good and bad qualities in his behaviour. A good counsellor is one who not only has the ability to recognize good positive aspects of the behaviour of the students, but also has the skill to encourage them. During the counselling sessions, the students often reveal behaviours' which are not according to the accepted social norms. Sometimes they are ashamed of their bad behaviour. Under such conditions, the counsellor can help by appreciating the good things done by the students, which will help them to develop positive attitude about their behaviour leading to their personality development.

Counselling and Other Aspects of the Guidance Programme

If we consider the guidance programme as a wheel, the central process is counselling. The other processes either stem from it or lead to it. The main processes of any guidance programme are as follows:

- Individual inventory
- Orientation
- Research
- Counselling and Placement
- Follow-up

Different Types of Counselling

The different types of counselling include educational, vocational and Personal-social counseling, Self analysis, psychological counseling, psychiatric treatment and psychoanalysis.

The self-analysis is based on non directive counselling which is based on the process of educational and vocational guidance. Then, in the continuum would be psychological counselling, psychotherapy, psychiatric treatment, psychoanalysis, and other therapies.

Counselling and Psychotherapy

Arbuckle regards counselling and psychotherapy as synonymous terms. When a therapist aims at restoring a state of good health, he follows the same process as the counsellor does in achieving the optimum mental growth of the individual. Both have nothing to sell, nothing to prescribe.

"When a person acts in the capacity of a therapist, his goal is not to dominate or persuade, but simply to restore a state of good health," says Robert W. White. This is exactly what the counsellor does to the students. They both do not give advice and force their viewpoints. Through verbal or non-verbal communications, the therapist alleviates emotional disturbances, changes undesirable behaviour, and encourages personality growth and development.

Counselling and therapy have become so interlinked, that a new service has come into being which is known as psychotherapeutic counselling, under which conscious effort is made to modify the socially maladjusted behaviour of a patient who knows that he is afflicted with a personality disorder, which is being rectified.

According to Ruth Strang, counselling and psychotherapy have much in common. All forms of therapies, in her view, aim to empower the patients to understand themselves, and develop the ability to cope with their personal problems and other adverse life situations.

Thus, it is difficult to distinguish between counselling and psychotherapy. One process merges into the other. However, the counsellor primarily focuses on making his/her clients aware of their actual situation and their environment.

Difference between Counselling and Psychotherapy

1. Counselling is for normal client, and psychotherapy is meant for patients who suffer from a high level of anxiety, or other psychiatric disorder.
2. Counselling is given in school and colleges, whereas different forms of psychotherapy are given in hospitals and clinical settings.
3. The main methods of counselling are personality inventory and case study; in psychotherapy, methods used are case study, projective techniques, drugs, etc.
4. In counselling, self-understanding is the goal, whereas in psychotherapy restructuring of personality is the main goal.

4
Counselling Approaches

There are different approaches to counselling. The setting or approach is according to the emphasis or direction given by the counsellor. It is the emphasis present in the counselling interview which tends to modify it as directive, non-directive, or eclective approach.

1. Directive Counselling
2. Non-directive Counselling
3. Eclectic Counselling

Directive Approach

The founder of directive approach was E.G. Williamson. This approach comprises direct counsel from the counsellor who leads, and controls the counselling interview. The counsellor directs the activities of the counsellee. This approach assumes that the knowledge and experiences of the counsellor enable him/her to solve the problems of the counsellee. The counsellor, however, does not force the counsellee to accept the solution given by him. But, she/he directs the thinking of the counsellee to the acceptance of the plan of action that the counsellor thinks will be better for him/her.

Counselling in such a setting tends to be comparatively short and purposeful, because the time is not spent on the counsellee thinking over the problem, and arriving at the decision. Directive approach is also called trait and factor approach, which means that counselling process consists of analyzing and identifying abilities, interests, and personality traits of the counsellee, and matching them with the demands of different situations, i.e. educational, vocational, personal, and social.

Directive counselling is problem-centered. The counsellor analyses the reasons behind the problems, finds out the solutions, and offers them to the client.

In directive counselling, the main assumptions are:

1. It is an intellectual attempt to understand the problem.

2. That even when an individual is maladjusted, he/she has the power to recover through learning process.
3. That the counsellor has the duty to use his/her superior knowledge and experience in assisting the client.

Steps in the Counselling Process

1. *Analysis*—Collecting information from different sources—autobiography, diary, cumulative records based on grades achieved over the years—about the client. It includes anecdotal records, peculiar information, and psychological tests (intelligence and personality for analysis and interview).

2. *Synthesis*—Putting together the above information reveals the student's behaviour. It includes information about assets, weaknesses, adjustment, maladjustment, etc.

3. *Diagnosis*—It helps to know the root cause of the problem. Any information about the positive and negative aspects of the personality is sought. The problem of the client is identified to begin with. Thereafter, solution is sought and provided.

4. *Prognosis*—It means predicting the future development of a particular student whose problem cannot be solved through counselling. For example, when a student has high aspirations, but a low intelligence level, he is unable to reconcile to this fact.

5. *Counselling*—It is a major process in which there is face-to-face interaction. After developing a rapport, there is a discussion on the problems. By giving appropriate information, the process ends.

6. *Follow up*—After the counselling process, the client goes for follow up session. The counsellor, at this stage, tries to evaluate the success of the total programme.

Main Techniques of the Counselling Process or Stages

1. *Establishing Rapport*—This is the first step in any counselling process. Establishing rapport means development of trusted relationship between counsellor and client.
2. *Cultivating Self-understanding*—Family background, interest, weaknesses and strength are assessed. Mental health is given priority for better performance. Openness at the mental level helps the counsellee to discuss freely what upsets him. With free discussion, the counsellee is enabled to set goals, develop good social behaviour, courage and confidence to inculcate, and implement the desired behaviour.

3. *Advice*—Plays a very important role in directive counselling.
4. Modes of Advising
   a) *Persuasive*—Coaxing to take certain decisions.
   b) *Direct*—Advising for particular things.
   c) *Explanatory methods*—The counsellor presents things logically, and helps the client to take decisions.
5. Carrying out the Plan in Proper Direction
   (i) *Referral*—Some cases are sometimes referred to other personnel for overcoming special problems. For example, speech defect in a student can be improved by a speech therapist.
   (ii) *Evaluation*—The counsellor evaluates his own process of counselling by reviewing its impact on the student.

Drawbacks of Directive Counselling

1. Qualitative data is lacking in directive counselling, as too much emphasis is given to objectivity by using psychological and educational tests, which are standardized, and can be scored quantitatively.
2. Due to the narrow scope for collection of data, diagnosis is also narrow and incomplete.
3. Due to lack of systematic approach, the procedures at times begin with synthesis, rather than with analysis.

Non-directive Counselling

Carl Rogers is the founder and leading exponent of this approach. It is client centered counselling. In contrast to the directive approach, it is based on non-directive approach, which assumes that every counsellee is capable of solving his/her own problem provided he/she is made aware of the problems. In this approach, the counsellor does not direct the counsellee regarding the plan of action. He/she plays the role of listener. The main purpose in this case is to encourage the counsellee to talk freely, so as to bring his or her repressed thoughts to the surface, thereby relieving his or her tension, leading to a better understanding of his/her problems.

The non-directive approach is particularly suitable when the counsellee's problem is emotional. The counsellee seeks the counsellor's help in a state of anxiety, worry, or tension. The counsellor enables the sufferer to approach the problem from a new angle to modify his/her attitude, and recognize his/her goals. It is evident that counselling of this kind is more time-consuming. The non-directive approach is also suitable for educational and vocational decision making.

Success of the process depends upon:

1. How far the counsellor puts himself in the position of the client.
2. How far he rephrases the emotional content of the client's remarks.
3. How far he enables the client to see himself more clearly and develop insight.

Stages of Non-directive Counselling

1. Defining the problematic situation
2. Free expression of feelings-in this client can express his feelings freely and counsellor approves this.
3. Development of Insights-
4. Classification of positive and negative feelings
5. Termination of counselling situations

Characteristics of Non-directive Counselling

1. It is a client centered counselling.
2. In this counsellor is passive to the maximum.
3. Its use reduces psychological tensions.
4. In this defensiveness falls down.
5. In this process psychological adjustment of client improves.
6. Client behaviour is considered more mature emotionally.
7. In this entire responsibility is of client.

Criticism of Non-directive Counselling

1. The counsellor can never be really neutral because when he rephrases client's remarks, he selects certain points for emphasis.
2. The background information about the client which the counsellor receives may not have a direct bearing on the problem.
3. That much of the talking done by the client is not significantly related to gaining self-insight.

Problems in Counselling Services

1. Lack of understanding on the part of teachers and parents.
2. Lack of professionally trained personnel.
3. Lack of funds.
4. Some types of counselling do not fit into today's Indian educational institutions.
5. Some psychological tests are not suitable in Indian context.

Differences between Directive and Non-directive Counselling

E.H. Williamson

S. No.	*Counsellor Centered— Directive*	*Client Centered— Non-directive*
1.	In directive counselling, it is assumed that no individual can achieve self-analysis objectively as he has limited capacity.	It is assumed that the individual has great capacity to solve his own problems.
2.	In this, problem solving attitude is more important.	In this, more emphasis is on feelings, emotions, and a more permissive atmosphere is provided to the individual to express him-self and release tension.
3.	Comparatively short and purposeful.	Takes more time to discuss, and to take decision.
4.	It is problem centered.	It is client centered.
5.	It studies the past more than the present to solve the problem.	It has little concern for the client's past, and attaches more importance to the present.
6.	In this, the counsellor directs the counsellee to think, and accept the plan of action.	The counsellee is motivated to think through the problem himself, until he arrives at a solution, or course of action.
7.	Less scope for freedom of choice or of action.	There is much scope for freedom of choice and of action.
8.	Identifies interests, abilities, and personality traits, and matches them with demands of different situations.	Useful for educational and vocational decision making

Eclectic Counselling

Eclectic counselling was founded by F.C. Thorne. This approach has been further developed by those who do not believe in the extreme perspectives of directive and non-directive counselling. The counsellor may use both the approaches viz. directive and non-directive alternatively, according to the needs of the counsellee during the process. The approach may be modified whenever the need for change is felt.

The eclectic approach recognizes the fact that individuals differ in terms of their needs, personality, and experience. Hence, only one approach of counselling cannot be appropriately applied to all cases. It is an accepted fact that listening to the problem of the counsellee is very effective in some cases; whereas in other cases, the counsellor may change the course of action, and provide the minimum guidance necessary for help. In general, problems related to education and vocational choices, the directive approach may be more practical. Whereas problems related to personal/social areas need to be tackled with the non-directive approach. Both the counsellor and the counsellee are equally active in this type of counselling.

5
Individual Counselling

When counselling is provided to an individual for a personal problem, or when an individual seeks solution for a specific type of problem, or requires some special information, it is termed individual counselling.

Individual counselling may be of several types—Introductory, Fact finding, Informative, Evaluative and Therapeutic.

Individual Counselling Process

Most of the clients are ignorant of their problems. However, the observations and behaviour of others towards them may make them realize that they have a problem, which needs to be resolved. Thus, they feel the need of a counsellor to deal with their specific problem. Sometimes they are referred by parents and teachers.

In a counselling process, the counsellor and client interact and get to know each other through formal meeting. Usually, the clients are quite nervous and confused at the initial stage. They may also fall short of words to express their emotions and feelings. It is the duty of the counsellor to encourage such clients, and help them to relax. At the beginning, the counsellor should clarify the following points:

(i) Frequency of meetings.
(ii) Exact timing of their meetings.
(iii) Their relationship—formal, informal.
(iv) The nature of intractions—confidential, non-confidential.
(v) Subject matter and scope of meetings.

Individual counselling can have the following process:

1. *Introduction*—To begin with, there is an introductory chat between the counsellor and the client. Majority of the clients go to the counsellor with only a vague idea about their real problem. They generally initiate the conversation with some general topic, and later come to the real problem.

The counsellor encourages the client to talk about himself/herself (personal details). Open questions often prove to be helpful at this stage.

2. Finding the real issues and problems becomes the major challenge

for the counsellor. The counsellor can ask some facilitative questions at this stage, in order to know the real problem in depth.

3. During the course of discussion, questions like, "what happened next?" or "how did you feel about that?" etc. may elaborate and focus on the real problem. However, at this stage it is difficult to make any quick judgement. It is difficult for the counsellor to cope with the feelings or emotions of the client in the beginning. The counselling process involves coping with feelings or emotions. As each individual responds differently, there is no set norm to deal with problems. Clients can be better served if their emotions and feelings are well accepted by the counsellor. The emotional release is natural as well as curative in nature. It helps in finding a suitable course of action. Counsellor should be neutral and should not be judgemental due to his own thinking and emotions.

A counsellor must always listen attentively and should try to encourage the expression of feelings or emotions by the client, as this is essential for the success and effectiveness of the counselling process.

4. *Finding a possible solution*—When the client expresses anything emotionally, he/she should be further encouraged to think, and find possible ways to confront, and solve his/her problems.

Sometimes an instant solution of each and every problem is not always possible. At this stage, the client is able to clearly identify the problem, and is motivated to find a solution to his/her problem in due course of time and develop coping strategies to resolve problems.

A brainstorming session helps this process in a big way. In this session, the client is encouraged to be constructive, spontaneous, and rational; the ultimate solution evolves from within these various solutions.

5. *Formalizing a plan*—Once the ultimate solution is identified, and accepted; there is need to formulate a feasible plan of action.

Counsellor and client work together in a synchronized manner in order to finalize and formalize a practical and feasible plan of action. While drawing up a plan of action, care should be taken to ensure that it is a workable plan, that it is reasonable, achievable, and practical.

6. *Plan implementation*—Usually, a plan is implemented by the client independently. What he/she needs is a particular plan, which is suitable to the problem, and can be implemented without anxiety. It is the duty of the counsellor to provide this type of assistance to the client.

7. *Evaluation and adjustment*—A plan is evaluated and adjusted according to the client's needs and requirements.

8. *The end*—At the end, when the plan has been implemented, and the problem sorted out; the relationship between the counsellor and the

client should come to an end. This is a very difficult process, as during the process of interaction, client gets emotionally attached. The counsellor needs to deal with this situation tactfully.

The client at this stage should also be given an opportunity to consolidate and build upon the skills learned during the coaching, and the counselling sessions.

Individual Counselling Tools

It can be done through interviews of different types.

Interview

It is a give and take of views between the interviewer and interviewee. It consists of consultation, mutual interchange of opinions, and deliberating together. It can be used to exchange information, and to change behaviour. It is done on the basis of free flowing manner in which discussions take place.

Interview Procedure

1. *Preparation:* It requires planning for satisfactory results. It decides what is to be accomplished

(a) Knowing interviewee through school records, from friends, parents, and teachers.
(b) Giving an appointment saves time.
(c) Providing privacy. There should be no interruption during the interview.

2. *Attitude:* The interviewer needs to be objective, not subjective.

The Process

(a) Establishing rapport with the client. There should be a relationship of trust, confidence, and mutual understanding between the two.
(b) Helping the interviewee to feel at ease, and become ready to talk.
(c) Helping the interviewee with appropriate information to choose the most suitable activity.
(d) Asking unambiguous questions.
(e) Learning to listen carefully.
(f) At the close of the interview, watching for additional information or new leads in the casual remarks of the interviewee.

Interpretation—without interpretation, the counsellee may remain on a superficial level of self-understanding. The interpretation to students of the varied aspects of their emotional life is essential. This requires great skills and understanding.

Developing insight and putting them to work—appropriate plan of action is required. The professionally successful interviewer is resourceful in making the counsellee reach his/her decisions and put them into practice.

Recording—This should be done properly and effectively. As tape recorder helps in getting complete records or summary can be written just after taking interview.

Behavioural Counselling

This is the most modern method of treating behavioural disorders. Behaviour counselling is based on the principle of conditioning reflexes, describing behaviour, and specifying the conditions under which it is acquired, maintained, and eliminated. Behaviourists argue that behavioural disorder is a problem, and not a systemic problem. Behavioural counselling is a technique based on the principles of learning. Important contributions have been made by Pavlov and Skinner in this field.

The success of behavioural counselling depends on:

1. Establishing valid hierarchy by the client and the therapist.
2. Discovering an adequate reinforcer by the therapist.
3. Lack of counter conditioning outside the therapy session.

In the first stage of the counselling process—in which counsellor and client come to know each other through formal meetings—usually clients are a bit nervous and confused at this stage. They may feel short of words to express their emotions and feelings. The counsellor encourages the client, and helps him/her to relax. Before actually arriving at a solution, the counsellor clarifies the following points:

(i) Frequency of meeting
(ii) Exact timing of their meeting
(iii) Their relationship—formal, informal
(iv) Their meeting—confidential, non-confidential
(v) Subject matter and scope of meeting

Process of Behaviour Counselling

1. *Introduction*—this involves introductory talk between counsellor and client. Majority of clients reach counsellor with only a vague idea about their real problem they initiate the conversation with some general topic and then come to problem.

Counsellor encourages the client to talk about himself/herself (personal details). Open question often proves to be helpful at this.

2. Finding the real issues and problems now the real problem comes in to surface. Counsellor can ask some facilitative questions at this stage, in order to know (details) of real problems.

For Example—

(a) What happened next?
(b) How did you feel about that?

These types of questions elaborate and focus real problem—at this stage it is difficult to take quick judgement.

3. Coping with feelings or emotions are a bit difficult to cope up for most of us. The counselling process involves coping with feelings or emotions—counselling very heavily concentrates on the emotional aspects of the clients. All human beings respond quite differently when taken as individuals as all individuals are different. And we cannot generalize that all people are different to do things differently or face real life situations differently.

Clients can be better served if their emotions and feelings are well accepted by the counsellor. The emotional release is natural as well as curative in nature. Emotional release is helpful and able to find a suitable course of action.

A counsellor must always listen attentively and should try to encourage the expression of feelings or emotions, by the client, as this is essential for the success and effectiveness of counselling process.

4. *Finding possible solution*—once a client experiences the emotional release he/she should encourage finding possible ways to confront and solve the problems.

The solution of each and every problem is not always possible. Some problems do not have any solution at all. At this stage the client is able to clearly identify the problem and try to find solution of his/her problem.

A brainstorming session helps this process in a big way—in this session, encouragement is given to the client so that they can think various possible ways of their problems—the client is encouraged to be constructive spontaneous and rational. Alongside this, client is also encouraged to be sensible, logical as well as thoughtful.

The ultimate solution evolves from within these various solutions.

5. *Formalizing a plan*—once the ultimate solution is identified and accepted, a need arises to formulate a plan of action, which is possible as well as feasible.

Counsellor and client work together in a synchronized manner, in order to finalize and formalize a practical and feasible plan of action—while drawing a plan, care should be taken to ensure that the plan works. Plan work; plan should be reasonable, achievable and practical.

6. *Plan implementation*—usually a plan is implemented either by the counselor or client together or independently by client i.e. on his/her own. The client only requires some plan to be decided by the counselor, sometimes its implementation brings changes which brings anxiety. So it is duty of the counsellor to support client wherever required and also suggest strategies in overcoming the present problem and also anxiety associated with that problem.

7. *Evaluation and adjustment*—plan is evaluated and adjusted according to client's needs and requirements.

8. *The end*—at this stage the relationship between counsellor and client should come to an end—this becomes emotional problems for both because both are human beings and attached. At this stage client should also be given an opportunity to consolidate and build up on the skills learned in coaching and counselling.

Problems requiring Group Guidance

We require group guidance for following kinds of problems:

1. Problems related to educational plans;
2. Problems relating to home and school adjustment;
3. Problems relating to social situations;
4. Problems relating to use of leisure time;
5. Problems relating to job findings;
6. Problems relating to personality;
7. Problems relating to economic and occupational activities;
8. Problems relating to hobbies.

Elements of the Counselling

According to Fiedler (1950), the following can be termed as the essential elements of the counselling:

1. An empathic relationship
2. The counsellor and the client relate well
3. The counsellor sticks closely to the client's problems
4. The clients feel free to say what they like
5. An atmosphere of mutual trust and confidence exists
6. Rapport is essential.

Techniques of Behavioural Counselling

I. Operant conditioning
II. Aversive conditioning

I. *Operant Conditioning*

Operant conditioning uses techniques such as positive reinforcement, punishment and modeling to help alter behaviour. The following strategies may be used within this type of therapy.

(a) *Token economies*—rely on positive reinforcements and commonly used for improving behaviour.
(b) *Contingency management*—is more formal approach and involves written control between the therapist and individual that outlines goals, rewards and penalties. This adds sense of accountability.
(c) *Modelling*—involves learning through imitation and observations. It helps individual something to aim for, allowing them to change behaviour to match their role models.
(d) *Extinction*—work by removing any type of reinforcement to behaviour.

Individual Therapy Goals, Frequency and Duration

In general goal of psychotherapy is to talk through mental health concerns and help clients heal, grow and move towards more productive, psychologically healthy lives. Good therapy is client driven; it takes 45-50 minutes. Sometimes problems resolved in a short term and sometimes it needs a long term therapy.

Approaches of Psychotherapy for Dealing with Behavioural Problems

1. Psychoanalysis and psychodynamics
2. Cognitive behavioural therapy
3. Interpersonal therapy
4. Humanistic therapy
5. Integrative therapy
6. Rational emotive therapy

1. *Psychoanalysis and Psychodynamics*

It is in-depth talk therapy that aims to bring unconscious deeply buried thoughts and feelings to the conscious mind so that the repressed experiences and emotions often from childhood can be brought to the surface and examined.

The aim is to release repressed emotions and experiences make the unconscious-conscious this method is called 'the talking cures'.

Psychoanalysis believes that childhood events and unconscious feelings, thoughts and motivation play a role in mental illness and maladaptive behaviour.

This treats depression, generalized anxiety, self destructive behaviour, phobias, and psychosomatic disorders. It is also known as insight-oriented therapy and focuses on unconscious processes as they are manifested in a person's behaviour. The goal is client awareness and understanding of the influences of past on present behaviour.

2. *Cognitive Behaviour Therapy*

It focuses on how your thoughts, beliefs and attitudes affect your feelings and behaviour. Cognitive Behaviour Therapy (CBT) aims to teach effective coping strategies for dealing with different problems throughout life.

It is used for anxiety disorders, phobias, social and generalized anxiety disorders. The process of this therapy takes around 5-20 weeks with each session of 30-60 minutes. It is most effective in moderate to severe depression.

3. *Inter Personal Therapy*

Inter Personal Therapy (IPT) is a method of treating depression. It focuses on its client and its relationship with other people. It is based on the idea that personal relationships are at the centre of psychological problems.

Depression is not caused by an event or relationship; however it affects relationship and creates problems with interpersonal connections. The goals of IPT are to help you communicate better with others and address problem that leads to depression.

In this therapy, therapist usually conducts an interview in which he identifies events in client's life that lead to depression. He tries and equips the client with required skills that help client to deal with difficult emotions in positive ways. IPT treats bipolar disorders, borderline personality disorders, mental disputes, panic disorders and substance abuse.

4. *Humanistic Therapy*

It is based on humanistic theory which emphasis hierarchy of needs and motivation. It is a client centered approach by helping clients to understand his/her own development. It looks at human behaviour, in this focus it works on the ways to help an individual to improve self-image and self-actualization the things that make him/her feel more worthy/important. It treats depression, anxiety, panic disorders, addictions, relationships issues including family issues and schizophrenia.

5. *Integrative Therapy*

It is the integration of elements from different schools of psychotherapy in treatment of clients uniting cognitive behavioural and physiological system within a person.

6. *Rational Emotive Therapy*

The rational emotive therapy was developed by Albert Ellis. According to him, a human being is both rational and irrational. Irrationality is the cause of emotional problems, such as guilt, anxiety, anger, and depression. Emotional problems cannot be separated from ideas. Ellis thinks that the mistakes most people make emanate from the rating they give themselves against other people, and then labeling themselves accordingly.

Ellis has identified different areas of irrationality, which lead to neuroses.

1. An individual has to be loved by every significant person in his environment.
2. Every individual should be competent to achieve in area/s of his interest.
3. Unhappiness is not within an individual's control.
4. Individuals are upset by problems of other people.
5. Individuals are always concerned with things which are harmful and dangerous.

The aim of establishing a goal of Rational Emotive Therapy is to show the client how his/her misinterpretations of events are causing him/her problems, and to teach him/her to see things in a more rational manner, and help in the process of adjustment.

Techniques used for Rational Emotive Therapy are persuasion, confrontation, challenge, command, and even theoretical arguments. They are directive in their approach for solving problems.

II. Aversive Conditioning/Therapy

This process pairs undesirable behaviour with some form of aversive stimulus with the aim of reducing unwanted behaviour. An example of how this is commonly used is when an alcoholic is prescribed certain drugs that induce nausea, anxiety and headaches when combined with alchohol, this means every time the person drinks, they get negative side effects, this hopes to put off that person from drinking to help them overcome their addiction.

6
Group Guidance and Counselling

Concept and Meaning

Group counselling is different from individual counselling. Group counselling is applied to groups. Many features of group counselling are unique, and it would be wrong to apply the same counselling methods to different groups or masses. A counsellor trained in the skills of individual counselling might find it difficult to conduct group counselling without appropriate training.

In group counselling, there is one counsellor who works with a group of students. Group processes are the preferred mode of working for dealing with people who have difficulties in interpersonal functioning or have common problems. There are limitless possibilities in counselling a group; whereas the demands of individual counselling are quite different, and much more challenging.

Group counselling allows greatest amount of learning for more people at a time. Group counselling is sometimes more successful with students who have not responded well to individual counselling. Group counselling is a particularly useful for helping adolescents for whom peer values are important. The interaction in a group requires adequate insight and understanding of the problems of other students by listening to their difficulties, or through discussion.

Difference between Group Guidance and Group Counselling

1. Group guidance is recommended for all individuals on a regular basis; while group counselling is generally recommended only for those who are experiencing some coping difficulties in their lives.
2. Group guidance makes an indirect attempt to change attitudes and behaviours; while group counselling makes a direct attempt to modify attitudes and behaviours.
3. Group guidance can be done with large classroom size groups;

whereas group counselling is most effective in small and groups with similar problems.

Group Counselling

It is one of the strategies of group guidance. Nature and principles of group guidance involves those activities within the organization of guidance programme, wherein several students meet, interact and gain information, share ideas, plan for the future, and take decisions.

The term group counselling is being applied to a variety of guidance services in small groups. Usually these small groups are formed in order to provide therapeutic services to individuals with special problems, and provide intensive help during almost any phase of guidance.

Group counselling is especially appropriate for adolescents. It enables teachers and parents to discuss the following problems of adolescents:

(a) Their discomfort, embarrassment.
(b) Intelligent use of good reading material.
(c) Ability to address questions seriously, and satisfy some of their strongest needs, especially in providing real assistance to peers while obtaining assistance from them.

Group Counselling Process and Preparation

Preparation for group counselling should take in account the following three concerns:

1. *The individual's own identity:* What kind of method would be best for him/her?
2. *The problem of choice:* How do people learn what they need to know? This becomes even more relevant when choosing between two or more contrasting methods.
3. *The problem of performance*: How much laboratory experience does one need to perform effectively?

The preparation or training of counsellors should be broadened and deepened.

1. They should have academic experience, emphasizing values and conditions, but also experiences related to human behaviour.
2. Information should be well organized.
3. The group counsellors should commit themselves to become genuine participants in the relationship with each member of the group during preparation and practice.

4. Group counsellors need to be sensitive and imaginative.
5. They must accept change, ambiguity, confusion etc. as part of life.

Besides, they should have experience of the following activities:

1. Literature and drama.
2. Philosophical and religious thinking that man's deepest communication is through symbols.
3. Experience of Art: Counselling at its best is an art. Although a person transmits thoughts by words, it is by art that feelings are transmitted. This is a function of art which is based on the capacity of a person to receive another person's expression of feeling, and to experience those feelings oneself. Art is a basic ingredient in interaction, growth, and development, and in life itself. Music has the power to stir emotions and bring comfort. It has a mysterious quality (music is to the mind what air is to the body).

Preparation of Group Counsellor

The counselling process can be short or long, depending upon the issues and problem. Since group counselling focuses on the meaning and issues of the life, a counsellor depends on the understanding not only of the related behavioural sciences, but also of philosophy, literature, art, and religion.

The counsellor is not only a scientist in the sense that he uses the insights and method of science, but is also an artist, making use of basic feelings and intuitions. Since group counselling is both science and art, different types of skills are involved. Any outcome depends not only upon the counsellor's knowledge and understanding, but also upon his/her unique performance. Since each counsellor's functioning depends on his uniqueness.

Each counsellor must take into account guidance, psychology, sociology, and anthropology to provide the theoretical foundations of counselling with groups.

The trainee counsellor participates in several seminars and workshops, designed to integrate his knowledge and understanding gained from art and science.

Counsellor should experience the meaning of group leadership and group membership. He learns the required skills by participating in group activities, which are necessary for involvement as a group member and group leader. These group experiences provide a basis for understanding group process, and for development of necessary skills which help him to take a tentative decision regarding his preference for group centered therapy and method. For this purpose, he can also use video tapes to observe various kinds of groups in action.

He should have internship experience of handling a group and its problems. The members of the group should be of certain age, and of a particular socio-cultural background, requiring professional counselling from the counselling.

Suggested Direction in Group Counsellor Preparation

Adjustment should be the goal of counselling. The training must be oriented to the whole person, and throughout his life.

Group counselling deals with one's whole life. Therefore, training needs experiences, not only within the scope of science, but also in the field of arts.

The counsellor should use different methods according to the needs and requirements of the group. The counsellor/educator should lay emphasis on the knowledge of theory and practice. He/she should also stress upon experience or some combination of these two. Theory is the knowledge attained through discussion of the various concepts, which is necessary in practice.

Principles of Group Counselling

1. The group should be homogenous.
2. Guidance offered should be of common nature, useful for all members, and universally applicable to all.
3. Individual problems should be discussed, and not ignored.
4. Group guidance should be followed by individual guidance wherever necessary.
5. Even in the group guidance, individual problems should receive attention to be resolved by proper guidance.

Aims of Group Counselling

1. Assist and identify common problems.
2. Provide information useful in solution of identified problems.
3. Provide opportunities for group thinking related to various problems and experiences.
4. Promote self-understanding and to lay the foundations of individual counselling.

Objectives of Group Counselling

The objective is to assist the counsellees in the following ways. Following are expected outcomes of group counselling:

1. Achieve increased maturity regarding realistic goals and adjustment.
2. Understand them, and achieve adequate insight of their fellow members.
3. Release the feelings of anxiety and frustrations.
4. Acquire learning by communication and interaction.
5. Utilize the different knowledge skills, abilities, and experience of group members to enhance their own.
6. Stimulate critical thinking.
7. Increase motivation of group members.
8. Express and clarify their own ideas.
9. Formulate and examine their own attitudes.
10. Make decisions and solve problems.
11. Apply and study group process, norms, and dynamics.
12. Develop a learning situation in which the members can achieve their objectives in the group.
13. Enhance oral communication skills.
14. Become less dependent on the trainer in managing their own learning.
15. Learn to take more responsibility for their own learning, and consequently to improve their preparation for it.

Need for Group Counselling

1. *Search for identity*—This is the central theme for individuals. They want to know who they are, what they can become. This gives them confidence, and the courage to face problems as they come, and to solve them.

2. *Increased understanding*—There should be increased understanding of the concerned individual's special interests and abilities, like aptitude, with the help of some special testing by the counsellor. Today's adolescents are better able to explore their real self, share their positive feelings about their strengths, and fears about their weaknesses. They should be able to accept weaknesses, and try to correct them, and adapt plans accordingly.

3. *Improved skills in obtaining adequate information*—Adolescents are seriously concerned about learning more about the opportunities

available to them, and to improve their understanding of their environment. In a counselling group, they feel free to ask questions and express their views. Within the safe atmosphere of a counselling group, they also enhance their own self-respect by helping others. The counsellor must encourage, and develop the feeling of genuine worth in the learners.

4. *Improved skills in assimilating and appraising information*—They must learn where to find validating information, and how to make decisions. For this, they can get the assistance of fellow clients. They should be able to discover, and understand why they failed; and what needs to be done to overcome the causes of their failure. It is very important that they understand their teachers for assimilating and appraising information. The counsellors should try to limit their discouraging behaviour and prevent their youthful team from making mistakes by citing their own example, instead of criticizing them. The teachers can take help from the counsellor to play their roles more effectively.

5. *Increased interpersonal skills, and confidence in one's ability to recognize and solve own problems*—Participation in counselling group and in open discussions in groups can have a great impact on adolescents. It can teach them how to relate openly, and to help others by closely observing non-verbal behaviour like body postures, facial expressions, and motor reflexes which reveal real feelings.

6. *Improved sensitivity, sympathy, empathy towards others' needs, and improved skills to help others*—These qualities are developed during the counselling process in the groups. During discussions, the adolescents reveal their inner feelings to the other people present there, like parents and counsellors, who listen to them carefully. This helps in solving many family problems to a large extent. It also gives an opportunity to parents to get more involved with their children, and act as role models.

7. *Improving relationship skills*—Learning in such groups can lead to improved skills to manage adverse situations.

8. *Independent behaviour can be observed, practised, and reinforced in a counselling group*—In a group, the constituent members learn from each other's views, and discover their own personal views. Suggestions and feedback help in improving one's behaviour. In such a forum, individuals also learn communication skill.

9. *Grooming knowledge and skills*—Learning how to cope with physical and emotional changes is also achieved in group counselling. In this meaningful interaction with admired and trusted peers, adolescents can learn to discuss their health, size, skin, aptitude, social development, etc.

General Functions of a Counsellor in a Group

1. Works for the benefit of the group.
2. Presents problems and issues for discussion.
3. Encourages internal communication and interaction between members.
4. Initiates new approach, ideas, and practice.
5. Retains group memberships.
6. Structures his work and group structure.
7. Creates a friendly atmosphere.
8. Facilitation for achieving group goals.
9. Rewards members with praise and recognition.
10. Evaluates work and progress of groups and individuals.
11. Encourages participation and decision making by the group and individuals.

Role of Counsellor in Group

1. Encourage students to recognize their own selves.
2. Help them to interact in group.
3. Develop a rapport with the participants.
4. Teach acceptance.
5. Listen attentively to all that each individual has to say.
5. Promote understanding, sympathy, and empathy.
6. Be a problem solver.
7. Know how to close a discussion or session.

Communication in Group Counselling

Communication should be authentic, real and honest. Involvement is a part of communication. Involvement at the cognitive, emotional, and neurological level is necessary for behavioural changes. However, communication is of little value for the purpose of group counselling, if it is too mechanical and superficial. Communication is frequently used merely as a token. It has definite maintenance value, and helps each of us to move through the mechanics of the day.

The utility of communication is beyond the token form, but its usefulness is dependent upon a deeper, more risk taking, and genuine form of relationship.

Spending time in a group to discuss facts, injustices, personal frustrations, intolerable personal relationships, dissatisfaction with one another, and appreciation for one another is of great importance for proper development of an individual's personality.

Conflict is a significant component of basic communication. In a group, productive conflict can improve situations.

Creative Handling of Conflict to Initiate Change for the Better

1. It is to be recognized that problems cannot be faced or solved without conflicts. Different feelings, different values, structures, and different ideas collide with each other for a better outcome.
2. People must accept the importance of others' feelings, values, and ideas. They must retain human dignity, respect the rights of others, regardless of their different behaviours, and points of view.
3. There should be trust among the members.
4. The group must honestly and openly examine the issues, and using their joint productive imagination, project different solutions to arrive at tentative decisions and plans in relation to the problem.

Appropriate communication leads to constructive change and development.

Dynamics of Group Counselling

It includes its Structure, Purpose and its Functioning.

Structure of Group Counselling

Definition: Structure is the arrangement or interrelationship of all the parts of a whole with respect to each other.

Purpose

1. Similarities and dissimilarities are noted down.
2. Structure is studied to understand its functioning, and to develop competence to change it. Attention is given to the relationship between parts; the nature, and purpose of this relationship; how and to what degree modification of a part would affect the whole.

Structure is a way of examining the complexity of group process. This can provide more information about the nature and relationships between various structures, ranging from rigid to very flexible, group productivity, the effect of structure on members' involvement, and relationship between degree of structure and change in behaviour.

Dynamics is derived from the Greek word 'dynamos' which means force. Therefore, it means forces operating within a group. The study of these forces is the subject of investigation of group dynamics, the conditions under which these forces operate, the consequences they have upon people and events, and the way they can be modified. The practical applications of group dynamics consist of utilization of knowledge about these forces for achievement of the sole purpose. Group dynamics is the result of the interaction between the leader and group members. Group members behave as they do because of their needs, attitudes, patterns of interaction, and skills on which they rely for communication. Each group member brings his/her unique self to the group processes.

Group dynamics is concerned with problems that group members face in working together, and with the ways of solving them.

Attitudinal Functioning

1. *Dimensionality*—Some members look at life chiefly from a unidimensional view point (one angle); others examine issues chiefly from depth or two-dimensional perspectives. They go deeper to examine possible causes and outcomes, and their own responsibility related thereto. Group counselling is most beneficial when the interaction exemplifies both directions.

2. *Humanistic patterns*—Some members look at situations from narrow perspectives. They accept conditions as they are. They have made their world comfortable by making it small, and by not getting involved in new areas. These members exist as a part of the whole. While others have a broad view.

3. *Openness of belief systems*—A member is influenced by both the thought and emotional components of the discussion. These components influence the process and condition of the outcomes. All belief systems serve as powerful sets of motives and conflict. The conflict requires a cognitive framework to know, and understand threatening aspects of realities. Members with open belief systems tolerate ambiguity well. They do not overreact to threat; and distinguish between authority figure and their ideas to evaluate a situation on its intrinsic merits. Persons with more closed belief systems are hindered by a pervasive feeling of threat, and dependence upon authority.

Those people who idolize security, and live their lives to increase it for themselves appear to be a depressive factor in the group. Security needs actually minimize their development as group members. For example, children are not sent far away from the village or home even for better schooling due to security concerns.

4. *Involvement*—The attitudes and needs of each participant are reflected in their involvement. Each involves himself/herself according to his/her needs. The members satisfy their needs by verbal or non-verbal participation. They use both the methods for their benefit. The extent to which each member uses one or the other method, influences the interaction and outcomes. As the member's sense of interdependence, unity, trust, and caring becomes an accepted fact, silence becomes increasingly more useful.

5. *Skills*—Quality of communication depends on skills. These skills vary from member to member, and only a few members appear to have the requisite skill for effective functioning. Many lack skills like listening, clarifying, linking, synthesizing, and summarizing.

6. *Listening*—Listening is a very important skill. It is important for the purpose of trying to help another to understand one's situation, and oneself. Since usefulness to the members depends upon the accuracy of their listening, it is important that they make reasonably certain that they have understood. Group counsellor adds another dimension to their listening. They not only listen, but try to understand their inner feelings and perceptions. In this way, they respond more meaningfully to one another.

7. *Clarification*—Clarity and understanding must prevail in group counselling. Clarification makes possible a creative searching and expansion of meaning. The counsellor who clarifies ideas will encourage the members to express their creative ideas in the formative stage. Through discussions, they improve understanding and capabilities. Only after clarification, can discussion move ahead to clearer ideas and insights.

8. *Reflection*—The purpose of reflection is to express the meaning of an idea. It is important to have ideas clearly expressed. Those ideas help in developing insights. The more accurate the reflection of the meaning, the more self-understanding the members attain. This increases breadth and depth of relatedness.

9. *Interpretation*—A reflection remains within the meaning of the member's response; an interpretation goes beyond presenting ideas which are not included in what members say.

Uniqueness of individual ego is ignored. It is assumed that the self-interest of an individual in the group will probably disappear by overcoming the cultural lag.

The linking function—the counsellor plays the linking function in the group. In order to relate the comments of all members, the leader studies the meaning of each comment, their interrelation with each other, and attempts to recognize the relationship of each new comment with the new one.

Summarization—it is the most difficult skill. A good summary plays a unique and important function in helping the group to recognize the basic idea they have discussed. It provides direction, and also aids them in planning further steps. The leader or member summarizes when he considers it to be helpful to the group. This task requires concentration and practice.

Conclusion—the counsellors should involve the members in diagnosing and improving their skills. Attention should be given to development of insight, with reference to those skills which are appropriate at various times in the group's progress. The counsellor can assist members to recognize and understand the relationship between their personality structures and range of skills. These skills require intelligent efforts.

Kind of Group Structure: Formal and Informal

Formal groups are created as per official authority so as to fulfill the desired objectives. Informal groups are formed by the employees as per their likes, interest and attitudes.

Sociometry—Structuring for play may differ from structuring for work among the same population. Structure is a complex concept. There exists in the group, a formal structure with fairly fixed ends, which may include rules, regulations, methods, and outputs. The informal structure is free, social, open, permissive, and is an outcome of the resultant interplay of these two. Regardless of the objectives of the group, a proper balance of formal and informal is necessary for best results.

The group counsellor can hardly escape being involved with the structure. In fact, in order to understand the process, he needs to study the structure. Both his failures and successes are to a significant degree an outcome of the relationships among the structural forces.

A certain degree, type, and extent of structure are basic requirements, even crucial to all group activities. In determining the kind of structure to be used, the leader must be intelligent regarding his own needs and skills. The leader must be certain that the kind of procedures he envisages for applications are acceptable to those he is responsible. There should prevail an environment of trust, freedom, and responsibility, and the members should be open and accepting. It is very important to generate trust among the members, rather than control the situation through dominance.

Methods of Guidance and Counselling to Deal with Groups

1. *Career Conferences*

(i) During career conferences, information is imparted about occupational and vocational opportunities. In schools, it also includes the function of investigation of occupational interests of school children.

(ii) Arrangements are made for experts to facilitate talks on different occupational fields.

(iii) Writing of reports.

(iv) Evaluation of career conferences.

2. *Psycho-drama*—Introduced by J.L. Moreno, it is used to explore emotional problems, conflicts and frustrations. Herein, an emotional problem is dramatized.

3. *Group Therapy*—Group guidance is conducted by guidance worker or counsellor. Group therapy is conducted by a psychologist or a psychiatrist. A group which has psychological problems seeks the help of a psychiatrist. The number of members is limited to five or six. The aim is to solve the group's emotional and behavioural disorder through discussion, meditation, and other means.

4. *Group Guidance Classes*—These are organized to provide guidance on interpersonal and inter-group relations, personal and social adjustment, educational and vocational planning, and orientation on school and college or world of work, and are known as guidance classes.

Practical Considerations of Group Counselling

1. Physical arrangement.
2. Time factor.
3. Composition of counselling group—homogenous, same age, sex, educational, vocational.
4. Counselling group—The best size of a group for counselling is 6-8 persons.

Advantages of Group Counselling

1. The leader is an expert in direct discussion according to needs.
2. The expertise of the trainer is available, and can be used for direct discussion.
3. Group consensus can be achieved.

4. Decision making skills, independent of trainer's (leader's) support, are fostered.
5. Independent problem solving skills are improved.
6. Creative thinking skill is encouraged.
7. Social skills are exercised and improved, as the members have to work together, if group is to be effective.
8. Group work promotes intellectual development and rational thinking.
9. Positive behaviour is enhanced, and trainers know that it is more rewarding.
10. Self-discipline is necessary to abide by group norms. Group learning is more effective compared to self-study.
11. Group guidance is employed in orienting students to the guidance services of a new school, or to new aspects of these services in their present school.
12. Occupational and vocational information is shared.
13. Group guidance can lead to the discussion of common problems of students.
14. Group guidance can be conducted in extracurricular students' activities.
15. Group guidance multiplies contact with students.
16. It helps in improving students' attitudes and behaviour.

Group counselling is sometimes successful with students who have not responded well to individual counselling. Group guidance is organized to prevent the development of problems.

Disadvantages of Group Counselling

1. Negative behaviour may predominate, especially over-domination by a few talkers.
2. Leading a discussion requires a change of role on the part of the trainer, and he/she may not relish this, or have an aptitude for it.
3. De-briefing may not take place because of lack of time at the end of the discussion. Much of the effectiveness of group work is thus lost.
4. *Discipline*—Problems frequently arise. However, some groups contain individuals who are hostile, aggressive, and emotionally disturbed. Aggression may be channeled into productive activity. These individuals need one to one relationship with a leader who can give them extra time, but this should not be done to arouse jealousy or rivalry in other members.

5. Most people want to achieve recognition, and avoid punishment. Therefore, group discipline will be effective only if along with freedom and clarity of goals, there is flexibility.
6. There could be apathy in the group when members don't have the opportunity to use their initiative, and take responsibility. The attitude of the counsellor should not be authoritarian.
7. Disagreement in the group may arise due to a rapid shift from initial orientation to action. It is very important to spend adequate time in bringing out facts. Some aspects involve personal values, which may give rise to disagreement.
8. The problem of consensus may arise from diverse bases, motivations, and meanings. They could arise from:
   a. Fear of leader's displeasure.
   b. Unwillingness to oppose the majority of the group.
   c. Weaknesses on the part of the members may lead to abrupt end of meetings.
   d. Sometimes problems arise due to compromise.
   e. The fringe members or rejected individuals are not accepted by other group members.
   f. Negative behaviour may predominate, especially due to over-domination by a few talkers.
9. Leading a discussion in group requires a change of role on the part of other members, but some members do not have aptitude for that
10. Group counselling is sometimes very difficult. It is not simply individual counselling, nor is it merely an economic use of counsellor time. Many features are quite unique—group counselling requires special training which includes theoretical and practical knowledge of group and individual counselling.
11. It is not a complete answer for all the psychological ills and needs.
12. Size of the group can become a demerit or a disadvantage.

The term group counselling is being applied to a variety of guidance services in small groups. Usually, these small groups are formed to provide therapeutic services for individuals with special problems, but they are also meant for intensive help in almost any phase of guidance.

Points to Keep in Mind While Organizing Group Counselling

1. Redirect discussion which has become erratic.

2. Try to link contribution to objectives.
3. Be prepared to use OHP and board when needed.
4. Summarize evidence, re-phrase, re-organize, and clarify contributions.
5. Show positive behaviour.
6. Try to counteract and counter-balance the negative behaviour of others.
7. Attempt to participate at all times.
8. Communicate clearly.

Problems addressed by Group Guidance

The following types of problems are addressed by group guidance:

1. Educational plans.
2. Home and school adjustment.
3. Social situations.
4. Use of leisure time.
5. Problems related to finding a job.
6. Personality issues.
7. Economic and occupational activities.
8. Hobbies.

7
Psychological Testing

Psychological Tests

According to Anastasi

> "A psychological test is essentially an objective and standardized measure of a sample of behaviour."

According to Freeman

> "A psychological test is a standardized instrument designed to measure objectively one or more aspects of total personality by means of samples of verbal or non-verbal responses, or by means of other behaviours."

Thus, a psychological test is an effort to quantitatively measure the various aspects of behaviour of the individual, in such a way, that we can make generalized statements about his/her total performance and behaviour.

Need for Psychological Tests

1. To help students to make a decision.
2. To enable the counsellor gain broad characteristics' of counsellee and uncover as many promising opportunities as possible for the counselee.
3. To enhance the clients' ability to make his own decisions.
4. To help teachers adapt teaching methods as per needs of students.
5. To help establish a homogeneous group.
6. To provide information for selection, classification, and distribution of clients, to serve primarily the interests of the particular administrative system.
7. To help in the selection of students for special schools, for the award of merit cum means scholarships for residential schools in the community.
8. Selecting students for admission to special institutes.

9. To help in the distribution of personnel in various branches of services.
10. To help psychological diagnosis of students.
11. To help in treating psychiatric problems.
12. To help in dealing with behavioural problems.

Use of Psychological Testing in Counselling

1. Secure accurate and reliable information about each student's abilities, interests, and adjustment problems in order to give him proper guidance and counselling.
2. Make use of test results for further performance.
3. Help students to arrive at decisions connected to planning their educational and vocational future.
4. Diagnosis of student's problems like social adjustment, growth, and development, or academic deficiencies.
5. Help them evaluate the outcomes of guidance and counselling to plan further remedial programmes.

Characteristics of Good Psychological Tests

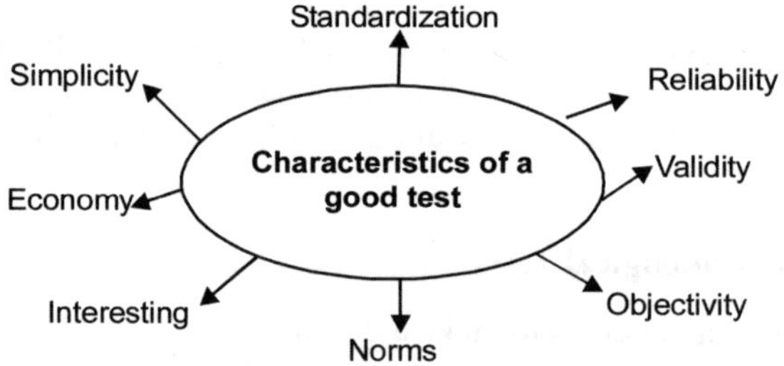

1. *Validity*—It means the degree to which the test actually measures what it proposes or claims to measure. It tells us what can be inferred from test scores. It is specific to the purpose, and the situation for which a test is to be used.

2. *Reliability*—It means the accuracy with which the test measures a particular trait, or it means the consistency of the results, or scores obtained by the same person when retested with the identical tests. Reliable tests, whatever they measure, yield comparable scores upon repeated administration.

3. *Objectivity*—Administration, scoring, and interpretation of scores should all be independent of the subjective judgement of the individual

examiner. The scores should be identical regardless of whosoever happens to be the examiner.

4. *Standardization*—It is used to compare different individuals.

5. *Norms*—All scores should be typical or characteristic of pupils or people of a given age or grade. A test must provide accurate norms in the form of age, grade, percentile rank, standard scores, etc. These norms would be meaningful for the purpose for which test is intended, or for group to be included.

6. *Simplicity*—Ease of administration, scoring, and interpretation is another important characteristic of a good test.

7. *Economy*—it should be possible to administer the test in a short time. This will help gain the cooperation of those being tested, and save time.

8. *Interesting*—Enjoyable tests encourage the examinees, and it be will possible to elicit the requisite information.

Testing in Guidance and Counselling

a) Use of Tests in Guidance, and Counselling—Intelligence tests, creativity tests, achievement tests, aptitude tests, interest inventories, and personality measures can be used to direct guidance and counselling in the right direction.

b) Administering—Scoring, interpretation, and analysis of test scores and communicating them is relevant in the context of a guidance programme.

Psychological Testing in a Guidance Programme

The individual is at the centre of guidance and counselling. No guidance programme can be successful without a proper study of individual. Psychological test facilitates in assessing intelligence, aptitude, interest attitude, personality traits, etc. These tests can predict future behaviour on the basis of present performance.

Uses of Psychological Testing in Guidance

1. *Making choices regarding educational courses to pursue*—Choosing the correct educational course requires matching results, talent, and levels of skills.
2. *Making choices regarding vocational courses to take up*—By predicting interest and aptitude in a specific area or skill,

educational choice if made properly then it will be more helpful in taking suitable vocational choices.

3. *Prediction*—It is helpful in making future prediction about chances of success in a chosen line of study or career.
4. *For career selection purposes*—Whether one wants to be in teaching, industry, or any other profession, you need to infer personality traits which will support the choice of career.
5. *Identification of personal and social problems*—Personality and other tests can indicate personal, social problems an individual is facing. For example, if a student is facing problem in interpersonal relations, a personality test can show if he is an introvert or has communication problem and so on.

Types of Psychological Tests

1. Performance test
2. Paper Pencil test
3. Individual test
4. Group test
5. Power test
6. Speed test
7. Standardized test
8. Non-standardized/Teacher made test
9. Verbal test
10. Nonverbal test

1. *Performance Test*—In these tests, examinees are required to perform a task rather than answering some questions. Instructions in these tests are given by using language as well as gestures. For example, different kinds of pictures are asked to be put in proper sequence. Examinee may be asked to make building or figure by given pieces of blocks. Generally the process is evaluated in these types of tests.

2. *Paper Pencil Test*—They are generally required reading and writing skills. Language is needed. Sometimes examinee may be asked to draw some picture or figure. Evaluation is done based on content provided as per requirement.

3. *Individual Test*—This test is administered to only one person at a time. Cube construction test or any type of performance test is the example of such test. If we examine the performance of more than one person at a time, no exact evaluation of the process will be possible, though evaluation of the person may be there at the end of the performance.

4. *Group Test*—These tests are administered to more than one person at a time. Group intelligence test and the achievement test are some examples. In these tests directions are so clear that no explanation is needed in the middle of the test.

5. *Power Test*—Sufficient time is given to answer all the items in this test, here items are arranged in increasing difficulty order and ability to solve all these questions are tested. Intelligence test is an example of power test. Speed test measures power when all the items are correctly attempted in the least time possible and power test becomes a speed test when easy items are correctly attempted in lesser time and the time thus saved is utilized to attempt difficult items. Once a time limit is fixed for a power test, it becomes a speed test.

6. *Speed Test*—In this test, examinee must answer all the questions of the test within time limit or in the shortest time possible. He should not commit any mistake while attempting or answering the item. Items included in such test are sequenced in difficulty level. Clerical aptitude test is an example.

7. *Standardized Test*—These tests must have gone through the procedure of standardization.

- There is a standard manner of instructions in these tests so that uniformity can be maintained in the standard of those who take the test.
- Reliability and validity of test are calculated.
- Norms for the test are also prepared.
- There are clear guidelines for scoring.
- These tests are constructed by specialists and they are administered and scored under uniform and standard testing conditions so that the results obtained from different samples may be easily compared.

8. *Teacher Made Tests*—They are constructed by the teachers who teach the class, or we can say they are specifically designed to rectify immediate classroom problems. The effectiveness of such tests depends upon the skill of the teacher and his experience of test construction. Rules for administration and scoring are also determined by the teacher. These tests are evaluated by the teacher himself. Achievement tests or examination paper are example of teacher made tests.

9. *Verbal Test*—Items in these tests require reading, writing and oral expression. Language is needed for communication here. Jalota's group intelligence test is an example. Such tests are called paper pencil tests

also because examinees are required a pencil and paper for expressing their ideas and knowledge.

10. *Non-verbal Tests*—Symbolic materials like figures, pictures, lines, etc. are used in these tests but instructions are given by using language itself. Ravens progressive matrices is an example of this test. These tests are used to measure special relationship or in those conditions when language may be a problem for the examinees.

What these Tests Indicate?

The performance test requires the manipulation of objects or mechanical apparatus; while paper pencil test requires the subject to record their responses on a prepared sheet. Similarly, the individual tests are administered to the subjects individually; while group tests are meant to be administered to individuals in a group.

Power test takes note of the limits of performing a specific task, and how much time is taken for its completion. Though the speed test involves elements of power also, it is required to observe how well the time limit is maintained. The non-standardized or teacher designed tests are not as expertly designed as the standardized or professional tests, however carefully they might be constructed.

Non-standardized tests are usually designed for specific groups of individuals, while the standardized tests are designed for more general use, and are considered ready for use.

The results are arrived at after:

1. A careful analysis of each item.
2. A careful analysis of total scores.
3. The establishment of their validity, reliability, and norms.

The setting up of uniform and objective patterns of administration, scoring, and interpretations is vital to establish the validity of any psychological test. Standardized tests are more commonly used as they are more reliable, have greater validity, and are more objective than the teacher made tests.

Limitations of Psychological Tests

1. Quantitative data of psychological testing are as definite, precise, and uniform as are the data of physical measures.
2. Classification of ability measures proves detrimental when assessed through the lens of quantitative data.

3. Psychological tests reflect cultural background, or social class. Hence, they are not valid or reliable instruments to measure ability.
4. The tests used in our institutions give a limited assessment of the students' capacity.

Intelligence Testing

Stoddard (1943) and David Wechsler (1944) define intelligence as:

> "Intelligence is the global capacity to deal effectively, think rationally, and act purposefully."

Therefore,

1. Intelligence is a general mental capability to address new problems, and face new situations in life.
2. Intelligence is the learning capacity of an individual.
3. Intelligence is the ability to think abstractly. It deals with symbols, numerical, and verbal problems.
4. Intelligence is a capacity to acquire and apply knowledge.

Kinds of Intelligence—abstract, social and mechanical

Characteristics

1. Intelligence is inborn
2. Impact of heredity on intelligence
3. Sex difference
4. Develops till adolescence stage
5. Helps individuals to solve complex and difficult problems
6. Individual differences in intelligence
7. Social, economic, and cultural factors affect the results of intelligence tests.

There is a deep relationship between intelligence and knowledge. The knowledge can be acquired with the help of intelligence, but the knowledge cannot help in the development of intelligence.

Theories of Intelligence

1. Binet's UNI factor theory
2. Spearman's two-factor
3. Thurston's multifactor theory
4. Group factor

5. Theory of primary mental abilities
6. Kelley's theory of intelligence

The ability to solve problems has been classified into two kinds of intelligence:

I. Intelligence quotient (IQ) measures rational or mental intelligence.
II. Emotional quotient (EQ) measures emotional intelligence.

Intelligence Quotient

Alfred Binet (1908) introduced the concept of mental age, to calculate the intelligence quotient of an individual. Mental age (MA) has been defined as the level of development in mental ability, which is characteristic of the chronological age (CA) at which any individual, on an average, arrives.

Generally, MA differs from the chronological age. It is noticed that the MA of a person increases with CA, but only up to certain limits.

$$IQ = MA/CA \text{ multiplied by } 100$$

An important characteristic of IQ is that it remains stable throughout the life of an individual with minor fluctuations. That is why IQ is considered as a reliable measure of human intelligence. The IQ level of average intelligence has been accepted to be 100. It means when:

1. If MA = CA, then IQ =100
   E.g. $16/16 \times 100 = 100$
2. MA > CA then IQ = above average
   E.g. $20/16 \times 100 = 125$
3. MA < CA, then IQ = below average
   E.g. $12/16 \times 100= 80$

Classification of Intelligence Quotient

Below 20	...	Profound
20-34	...	Severe
35-49	...	Moderate
50-70	...	Mild
71-90	...	Slow learner
91-110	...	Average
111-125	...	Fast learner
126-140	...	Intelligent
Above 140	...	Genius

Characteristics of a Well-Developed IQ

1. Adaptability in new situations.
2. Ability to differentiate between good and bad.
3. Effect of environment and hereditary.

Classification of Intelligence Tests

1. *Individual test or performance test*—Picture arrangement test, picture completion, maze test, cube construction, Alexander pass along test, and Peale's block test.
2. *Group test*—Army alpha test, army beta test, army general classification test, Terman group test of mental maturity, Dr. Sohan Lal group test of intelligence, and Prayag Mehta's general intelligence test.
3. *Power and speed test*—Grouping of easy to difficult items.

Measurement of Intelligence

1. *Pre-Binet Period*—Francis Galton, in his book, Hereditary Genius, demonstrated that personal characteristics (mental and physical) of men are inherited. He developed a series of tests to measure these characteristics.

2. The first laboratory of experimental psychology was established by Wundt in 1879 in Leipzig. Many of Galton's ideas were brought to the USA by an American psychologist J.M. Catell. Like Galton, he also believed that intellectual functions can best be measured by the reaction time and sensory discrimination tests.

3. The word Mental Test was first used by Catell in 1890 but his tests were actually tests of sensory discrimination, speed of motor responses and like.

1. *Binet Period*—Binet and Simon developed a variety of paper-pencil tests in their psychological laboratory established in 1889, to administer them on children of different ages. Through these tests, Binet tried to measure more complex mental functions such as power of judgement and reasoning, memory, and arithmetic abilities, etc. They developed separate test for different ages.
2. The concept of mental age was also developed by Binet and Simon for the first time in the history of mental testing; with this test, intellectual ability of an individual could be assessed.
3. *Binet-Simon scale*—The first scale of Binet-Simon was

published in 1905. This scale consisted of 30 items arranged in an increasing order of difficulty. This scale was a crude measure of intelligence of school-going children. In order to remove some of its defects they revised the scale in 1908. It was the first age based scale. The items in the tests were grouped according to the appropriate age levels from 3 to 13 Years.

4. 1908 revision of Binet-Simon Scale was adopted by many psychologists of America, Switzerland and Germany and many suggestions were given by them for the improvement of the scale. Binet and Simon accepted their suggestions and revised their scale again in 1911.
5. L.M. Termann of Stanford University revised this scale in 1916 to adapt to American situations. He introduced one new concept which was Intelligence Quotient (I.Q.) in his revision.
6. 1937, *revision of Binet-Simon Scale*—Terman along with his associate Merill revised 1916 scale again in 1937. The revision had two equivalent forms L and M.
7. *LM form revision of 1960*—Binet-Simon Scale was last revised in 1960 in which items of both L and M forms were included in the scale. In this revision, intelligence is expressed in terms of standard score of the deviation I.Q.
8. *Wechler scale*—This scale was considered as an improvement over Binet-Simon scale as it can measure the intelligence of adults very effectively. David Wechler developed this scale in 1939. Later on it was revised in 1955 and was renamed as Wechler Adults Intelligence Scale (WAIS).
9. *Post-Binet Period*—The following tests were developed after post-binet period.
   1. Cattells Culture fair test
   2. Large Thorndike's Intelligence test
   3. Ravens' Progressive Matrices test

Use of Intelligence Tests in Educational Guidance

1. To know the I.Q. level of subjects.
2. To help in choosing different curriculum.
3. To know the probability of any student's success and failure.
4. To diagnose the student's areas of difficulty.
5. To know the student's learning abilities.
6. Help in selection of course and career.
7. Help in classification of homogeneous group.

8. Help in diagnosing the causes of gaps in educational background.
9. Help in selection of candidates in officers' training.
10. Help in guiding educational and vocational choices

Creativity

It refers to original, novel thought processes which are grounded in reality. The process of creativity ensures originality, rationality, and usability. It must serve the purposes for which it is used. Those who are schizophrenic can make up original stories, but these don't have rationality.

Characteristics of Creative Individuals

Flexibility—those who are creative, are not rigid or inflexible in their ideas.

Fluency—their creation of ideas are more fluent and imaginative; e.g. Use of old bangles to create a picture, or using magazine cuttings to do so etc.

Originality—their ideas are original as they don't try to replicate the past.

Difference between Creativity and Intelligence

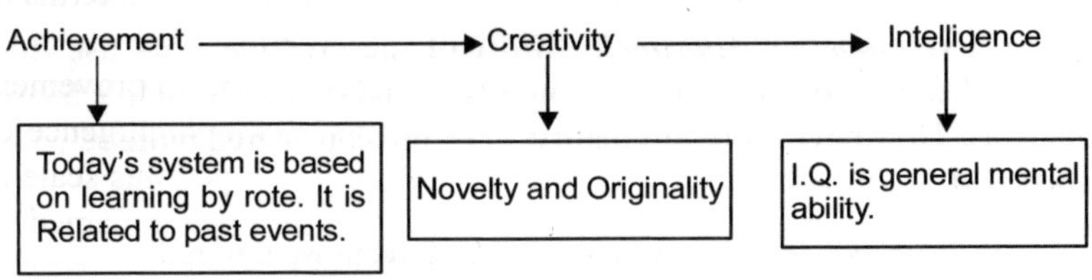

Relationship between I.Q. and Creativity

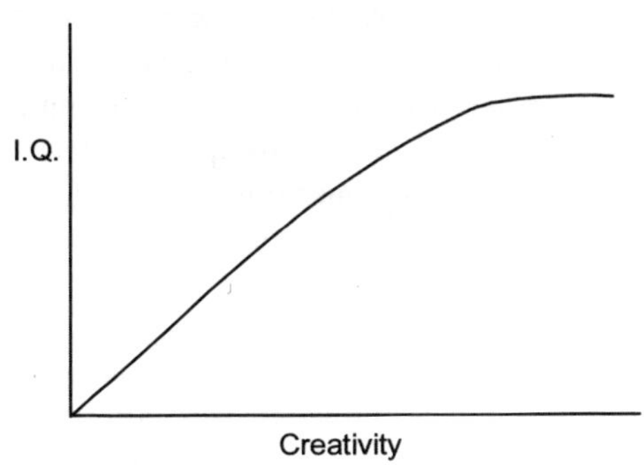

This is a curvilinear relationship between creativity and intelligence. It means that to some extent I.Q. leads to creativity, but only up to certain limits. A certain amount of I.Q. is necessary for creativity.

Approaches to Assess Creativity—Tests Based on Them

1. *Associative Approach*—one word is associated with another one. Like Remote Word Associated Test (RWAT), Rorschach Ink Blot Test, and Thematic Apperception Test (TAT), these are all projective techniques used both for assessing mental state and creativity of any individual.

2. *Cognitive Approach*—Certain cognitive styles decide the level of creativity.

Witkin's divides two styles as:

(a) *Centration*—Field dependence leads to responses which stick to specific objects. Their responses depend on the dominant aspects of stimulus.

(b) *Decentration*—Field independence takes them away from the given field. The responses are not within field as they think more creatively. Therefore, they are considered more creative. Like Witkin's figure embedded test.

3. *Psychometric Approach*—Most of the creative tests use this approach as they use statistics, are objective, and standardized like factor analysis. They have more rationality. They are considered more reliable and valid.

(i) *Torrence test of creativity*—One of the most common tests used to assess creativity in a child or an adult is series of figural exercises (thinking with pictures) and verbal activities (thinking with words) that students do to showcase their creative abilities.

(ii) Passi's test of creativity based on both quality as well as quantity. It include six sub tests namely: 1. The seeing problem test; 2. The unusual test; 3. The consequences test; 4. The test of inquisitiveness; 5. The square puzzle test; and 6. The block test of creativity. It measures three components of creativity—fluency, flexibility and originality.

(iii) Mazumdar creativity test based on the Guilford model of intellect

(iv) Bakar Mehndi verbal test of creative thinking includes four sub tests: consequences, unusual uses, similarity and product improvement test. It provides three factor score—fluency, flexibility and originality. It is available in both versions English and Hindi.

Aptitude Testing

For educational and vocational guidance of individual students, the knowledge of aptitude is very essential in helping them in making choices.

Definitions of Aptitude

W.V. Bingham defines Aptitude as, "A condition or set of characteristics regarded as symptomatic of an individual's ability to acquire with training some knowledge, skills, or set of responses such as an ability to speak a language or ability to produce music."

These conditions he regards as potentiality. Bingham emphasizes in the study of aptitudes that:

- An individual's potentialities are not all equally strong.
- Individuals differ from one another in their potentialities.
- The third hypothesis states that the pattern of aptitudes possessed by a person remains nearly the same. For example, a person who possesses a strong aptitude for teaching, but a very weak aptitude for school administration and organization, cannot become successful as the principal of a school despite receiving training in administrative practices.

Freeman regards aptitude as an indicator of an individual capacity to acquire with training some specific knowledge, skill or a set of organized responses such as the ability to speak a language to become a musician to do mechanical work.

Purpose of Aptitude Testing

1. Help in proper choice of course and career
2. Predict future success
3. Help the students in the development of social traits
4. Supplement other psychological testing

Why Aptitude Testing is Needed in Guidance

Taxler points out that aptitude is "a present condition which indicates individual's potentialities for future". On the other hand, Arthur J. Jones thinks, "Aptitude is not ability, but it is possible to predict about the future growth of a few abilities."

B.F. Skinner says, "Aptitude is comprised of special skills knowledge and interests."

It is vital to keep in mind that aptitude is specific mental ability which consists of mechanical, vocational, and artistic ability. In contrast, intelligence is general mental ability.

Aptitudes and interest are both responsible for the success and failure of any task.

Types of Aptitude

There are various aptitudes which have been identified. Some of these are mentioned below:

1. Aptitude for manual occupation
2. Clerical aptitude
3. Teaching aptitude
4. Musical and artistic aptitude
5. Medical aptitude
6. Legal aptitude
7. Mechanical aptitude
8. Aptitude for highly skilled occupation.

Clerical Aptitude

Clerical aptitude has four basic components—perceptual, intellectual, mathematical, and motor. Generally they are comprised of a number of sub tests including Verbal Reasoning Ability, Numerical Ability, Clerical and Spelling checking, etc.

Clerical Aptitude Test in India

1. Clerical ability test developed by Mysore University.
2. Clerical aptitude Test battery by educational and vocational instruction Bureau, Patna.
3. Parsi Panchayat Instruction Bureau, Bombay developed clerical aptitude test.

Options to Test Clerical Aptitude

1. Minnesota vocational test for clerical workers
2. National Institute for Industrial Psychology
3. Thurstone's examinations in clerical work
4. Detroit clerical aptitude examination

Mechanical Aptitude

1. Minnesota mechanical aptitude test
2. Johnson O'Conner's blocks tests.
3. O'Rourke Mechanical aptitude test
4. S test for mechanical aptitude
5. Scientific aptitude test developed by B.M. Dave in 1964

Components of Mechanical Aptitude

1. Scientific comprehension
2. Mechanical reasoning
3. Mathematical ability
4. Place related
5. Scientific information
6. Differential aptitude test (D.A.T.) developed by George K. Binet, Harold G. Seashore and Alexander G. Wesman

Sub-tests

1. Use of English
2. Clerical aptitude
3. Knowledge of mathematics and aptitude
4. Knowledge of science and aptitude
5. Mechanical comprehension
6. Oral reasoning
7. Group reasoning

Battery of Mechanical Aptitude Test by Psychological Lab, Allahabad

They ask the following activities for testing.

1. To assemble part of particular machine.
2. To put the correct blocks in the given board.
3. To ask questions related to application of machine parts.
4. To test ability of solving question related to geometry.
5. To ask insightfull questions related to physical and mechanical aspects.

Uses of Aptitude Testing

1. Aptitude testing are used for the purpose of predicting future success both in Educational and Vocational fields.
2. These test are used to help the students in proper choice of courses, subjects and careers.
3. They are used as they supplement other psychological tests.
4. Aptitude test is used to help the students in the improvement of certain special traits.
5. They are used for the purpose of admission and selection of students in the colleges and technical institutions.

Difference between Aptitude, Skill, and Proficiency

M. Mukherjee differentiates between skill and proficiency thus:

Skill is the ability to do job with care and perfection.

Proficiency is an individual's comprehensive ability, including not only an ability or competence in language, but also in book keeping, history, economics, and mathematics, or in any other activity.

If a person has an aptitude, at present he has a capacity, but not proficiency.

Jones says that achievement is related to what happened in the past; ability is related to the present; and aptitude is related to the future.

The above definitions indicate the following characteristics of aptitude:

1. An aptitude may be inborn or acquired
2. An aptitude may be constant and changing
3. An aptitude may be unilateral or multi-dimensional

Measures of aptitude like mechanical, electrical, teaching, and nursing have been designed, and are widely used in different places to provide educational and vocational guidance and counselling.

Tests of Spatial Ability

Mechanical Aptitude Test

It is supposed to involve sensory and motor capacities, and perceptual and spatial abilities.

1. Minnesota Spatial Relation Tests
2. Finger Dexterity Test by Johnson O'Conners
3. Mechanical Aptitude test by Stenquist
4. Mechanical Aptitude tests by O' Rourke's.

General Aptitude Test Battery

Clerical Aptitude Test—It involves speed and accuracy in perceiving numerical and verbal similarities; skills in spelling, usage, vocabulary, handwriting, and arithmetic, etc.

1. Minnesota Vocational Test for clerical workers
2. The National Institute of Industrial Psychology clerical tests

Test of Aptitude in Music and Art—Harold G. Seashore measures musical talent by taking into account the musical abilities of students of Class IV till college level. These measure the following musical abilities: speech discrimination, intensity or loudness discrimination, time discrimination, discrimination of sound, judgement of rhythm and total memory.

Test of Scientific Aptitude—It was created by D.L. Zybe for testing aptitude in different branches of engineering, and sciences like chemistry, physics, biology, and other work where success depends in part upon the ability to profit by training in scientific method.

Vocational Aptitudes

Tests of Medical Aptitudes: The study and practice of medicine require skills like reading X-rays, judging the colour of throat, palpitating for lumps, using surgical instruments, etc.

Differential Aptitude Tests (DAT) are likely to be useful in some specific set of occupations. They consist of the following sub-tests created by George K. Bennett:

1. Verbal reasoning
2. Numerical ability
3. Abstract reasoning
4. Spatial relations
5. Mechanical reasoning
6. Clerical speed and accuracy
7. Language usage—spelling
8. Language usage—sentence.

Interest Testing

Interest—Interest may refer to the motivating force that impels us to attend a person, a thing or an activity or it may be the effective experience that has been stimulated by the activity itself. In other words interest can be the cause of an activity and the result of participation in that activity (Crow and Crow, p. 248: 1973).

An interest is a tendency to become absorbed in an experience, and continue it.

Types of Interest

1. Manifest interest
2. Expressed interest
3. Tested interests
4. Inventoried interests

Characteristics of Interests

1. Interests are part of our personality.
2. Interests are inborn (inherited), or acquired (environmental).
3. Aptitudes affect interests.

4. Variation in interest decline with age.
5. Interest is related to feelings. Therefore, objective measurement is not possible.
6. Interests are temporary, changing with time and age.

Measurement of Interests

Educational and vocational guidance can be given only after assessing interests.

1. In 1919—first Interest seminar was conducted by Yoakum and first standardized Interest Inventory at the Carnegie interest inventory.
2. In 1921, Moor tried to measure the mechanical and social interests of engineers.
3. Kunder's preference records 168 items. Every item has three choices. Individuals select them according to their preferences.
4. Strong's vocational interest blank in 1927 by E.K. Strong—it contains 420 items related to vocational interest activities, school subject, personality characteristics. For scoring, scoring key to be used. The original test was designed only for men; a version for women was developed in 1933. In 1974, the Strong was merged into Strong Campbell Interest Inventory, which was further revised in1981.
5. Cleeton's Vocational Interest Inventory—630 items for which participants have to respond with 'Yes' or 'No' (9 parts).
6. Hepner's vocational interest quotient.
7. Thurston's interest schedule.

Interest Works in Two Ways for Guidance

1. It is important to find out the relation between individuals' interests and ability. Accordingly, interests should be cultivated for further development.
2. Selection of vocation according to interest.

Purpose of Interest Testing

1. To help the trainer and counsellor with information regarding students' interests to acquire a better understanding of students, and their problems.
2. Knowledge of interest helps to choose appropriate work and career options which would be sustainable in the long run.
3. Helps in making choice regarding apt educational vocational plans.

4. To help in channelizing energy of youth in some constructive directions.
5. To know the students' academic and vocational interest and thereby save them from frustration, stress and unhappiness to make them productive members of society.

Interest and Aptitude

While aptitude is a capacity or potentiality to acquire proficiency with a given amount of training; interest is merely a tendency to be absorbed in an activity, and to be attentive to it. Bingham holds that interest is a vital constituent of aptitude. If we have an aptitude for a vocation; it means that we have an interest in it. Aptitude for a vocation is more significant than interests. In choosing one's occupation, one should make sure that one has an aptitude as well as an interest in the work.

Aptitude might be a source of interest. Interest is a very complex psychological phenomenon. So many factors go into its making that it is extremely difficult to measure it accurately. There have been psychologists who declared that interest is not a measurable thing. But still, efforts have been made to measure interest objectively.

Objective Measures of interest

These measures include interest inventories. They contain questions which throw light on the likes and dislikes of individuals, their plans for the future, educational, and vocational interests.

Subjective Measures of Interests

This includes interviews, observation, achievement, and teachers' views. But the most practical method of assessing the interest pattern of an individual is the application of objective tools—i.e. interest inventory and blanks. The first such inventory was made in 1919. The following tests are most common:

1. Strong's interest inventory for vocations
2. Kuder's preference records
3. Thurston's interest inventory
4. Dunlop's academic interest blank.

Uses of Interest Inventories

By knowing the interests of an individual, it is possible to provide useful guidance. Interest inventories serve to improve teaching-learning situations, as well as in solving problems encountered in classroom related to maladjustment, etc., since they provide beneficial guidance to the teachers during classroom teaching.

Some Interest Inventories

(i) Strong-Campbell interest inventory (SCII) Developed by Strong and Campbell
(ii) Vocational interest inventory developed by N.D. Badami
(iii) Occupational and vocational interest record
(iv) Chatterji's Non-language preference record
(v) The interest test developed by S.P. Kulshreshtha
(vi) Thurston's interest schedule

Personality Testing

Definition of Personality—Allport G.W. 1948 defines personality as, "Personality is a dynamic organization within the individual of those psycho-physical systems which determine his unique adjustment to his own environment."

Factor Affecting Personality: Hereditary, Environment.

Differences in Personality according to Different Scholars

A. Hippocrates—Differentiated on the basis of disposition:

1. Sanguine (cheerful)
2. Choleric (irritable)
3. Melancholic (depressed)

B. Kretschmer (1925)—Differentiated on the basis of physique

1. Pyknic
2. Asthenic
3. Athletic

C. Sheldon's Classification—In his 1954 book, *Atlas of Men*, Sheldon categorized body types as Somatotypes and associated them with certain personality characteristics:

1. Endomorph
2. Mesomorph
3. Ectomorph

D. Jung—Proposed and developed the concepts of the extroverted and introverted personality, archetypes, and the collective unconscious:

1. Introvert
2. Extrovert

E. Spranger's Classification—Sorts humans by six basic cultural values:

1. Cognitive
2. Aesthetic
3. Economic
4. Religious
5. Political
6. Social

Watson J.B., 1930—Personality is the sum of the activities that can be discovered by actual observations over a long enough period of time to give reliable information.

Personality testing is necessary to achieve the following purposes:

1. Help the students in making proper educational and vocational choice.
2. Help the individuals in resolving emotional conflicts.
3. Help the teacher and counsellor in guidance situations.
4. Help the employer in proper selection of personnel.
5. Help the clinical psychologists in psychoanalysis and treatment of patients.

Projective Techniques of Personality Testing

T.A.T. (Thematic Apperception Test)—This test was developed by Murray and Morgan. This test contains picture cards. An individual while perceiving these cards projects his/her emotions and personality related characteristics. It contains 30 cards, 10 cards for females, 10 for males and another 10 are for both males and females, and uses 10 cards at a time. A person has to write a story in a given time based on that card. In this way he projects his own story, feeling, emotions and ideas in that story.

While analyzing, story is considered as whole instead of parts, proper interpretation of stories requires a trained personnel.

C.A.T. (Children Apperception Test)—It was developed by Dr. Leo Pold Bellak; this is for children aged between 3 to 10 yrs. This test consists of 10 cards, with different pictures of animals. Children are asked to write a story based on these cards presented one by one. Interpretation requires proper training and skills.

Rorschach Ink Blot Test—It was given by Swiss psychologist Hermann Rorschach. It contains 10 cards with ink blots, first five cards of black, two are black and red and last three of different colours. Investigator notes down the responses of examinee after presenting each card one by one. Analysis and interpretation is based on the responses, location, contents, originality and determinants, which requires a trained person, things, knowledge and experience of conducting these types of tests.

Sentence Completion Test—This test includes a long list of incomplete sentences. Testee is asked to fill the sentence immediately without thinking or taking extra time, they are considered better than word association test. It includes sentences like:

1. I wish ....
2. I feel proud when I ....
3. The aim of my life is ....
4. My ideal is ....

The projective techniques like TAT and CAT are generally used for mentally sick people.

Difficulties in Personality Testing

1. Subject's reluctance to disclose information.
2. Sensitive subject matter—Since the privacy of an individual is invaded, necessary precautions should be taken while interpreting the scores of intelligence and personality tests.

Non-Standardized Methods of Testing

1. *Interviews*

(a) Structured
(b) Unstructured

Interview is the basic, and most dependable, technique of counselling. It is useful to collect information, help counsellees to understand themselves, and to develop an insight into the overall situation.

Interview permits flexibility, clarification, explanation of certain points, and an opportunity for observation to the sensitive and trained eye of the counsellor. Interview is preferred over questionnaire in counselling process, as it provides the counsellor with an opportunity to study and understand the counsellee better.

A counsellee comes to a counsellor with mixed feelings of regard, and hesitation. A proper interview develops confidence in the counsellor by overcoming resistance, and communicating with her/him freely.

Every interview needs to have a definite purpose in view, and must be structured according to this purpose. The counsellors need to be sure as to how they are going to initiate it, and what responses are possible/ probable to the opening statements. In order to fulfill objectives, the interview has to be structured appropriately in advance.

Before this, the counsellor needs to establish rapport with the counsellee. Rapport is the relationship of confidence, trust, and mutual appreciation which helps the counsellees to express themselves without any hesitation and resistance. If the counsellor has an attitude of acceptance, sympathy, and concern for the counsellee's problems, then the counsellee can gain confidence, feel at ease, be willing to seek help from the counsellor, and confide problem. This is a good beginning for the process of counselling.

Another important thing which a counsellor must keep in mind is that a few leading questions should be asked to give a chance to the counsellee to express herself/himself. One of the important qualities which a counsellor needs to develop is the art of listening to others. A person who is too fond of talking makes a poor counsellor. This is the reason why many counsellors think that a teacher makes a poor counsellor.

Professional training of counsellor involves extensive practice with interviews, as this requires the use of appropriate words, right expressions, and emphasis. The use of devices like tape recorder helps the trainee to get feedback for the further improvement. A great deal of information can be collected from other sources rather than just the client; like from parents, friends, teachers, and other counsellors.

One major drawback in interview is the interviewer bias. Researchers have pointed out that the interviewers report a particular phenomenon according to their own interpretation, understanding, beliefs, and attitudes.

It has also been brought out through research that a skilled interviewer is also able to achieve a higher correlation between the interview and actual behaviour, than the unskilled one.

2. Observation

It is a method of collecting data. It is a process in which a person observes behaviour to note changes in people and places. It is learning through learning and documenting. Observation is most common in psychology and social sciences.

It involves watching a participant and recording relevant behaviour for later analysis. It is a method used in field of psychology to observe, describe, explain, predict and sometimes correct behaviour. Behavioural assessment is useful both in clinical and educational settings.

Modes of Observation

1. Participant observation
2. Structured Observation
3. Field Experiment

Methods of Observation

1. Testing method
2. Case study method
3. Cross sectional method
4. Naturalistic observation method
5. Laboratory method
6. Longitudinal method.

3. *Self-rating and Personality Inventories (Paper and Pencil Personality Tests)*

Individuals' written account of the past behaviour feelings and wishes can be a good source of information about their personality.

For example, Bell's adjustment inventories—a. adult; b. students; c. areas of adjustment social, home, health, emotional.

(i) *Minnesota multiphasic personality inventory (MMPI)*—this consists of 550 affirmative statements in which examinee is given options of true, false responses.
(ii) *P.C. Cheung's multi-trait personality inventory (MTPI)*—yields scores on 8 personality scales.
(iii) *Self-analysis form by R.B. Cattle*—there are 40 questions, dealing with difficulty that most people experience at one time or another.
(iv) *Adjustment inventory by H.S. Asthana*—this can be administered with groups and individuals. It is meant for high school and college students.

4. *Checklists*

Items are given to students (subject) who are asked to check the items which are applicable to them, e.g. 'I easily make friends,' 'I am careful about my things'.

A checklist is a type of questionnaire, in the form of a set of items which the respondent is asked to check. A checklist can be arranged in any of the following ways:

(a) The form in which the respondent is asked to make a check mark (") in the blank provided against each item. Example: Make a check mark (") in the blank provided against each activity undertaken in your school—
- Scouting
- School parliament
- Gymnastics
- Photography
- Games and sports
- Gardening

(b) The form in which the items with a 'yes' or 'no' are asked to be encircled, underlined, or checked.
Example—Does your school has a parent teacher association? Yes/no.
1. The forms in which items are in positive statements with checks (") to be put in a space provided on the right before the positive statement.
Example—The school has a student union. (")
2. The form where items are given in the form of sentence, and the appropriate word in the sentence is checked, underlined or encircled.
Example—The dramatic club meets—weekly, monthly, irregularly.

Analysis and interpretation of checklist data—The same processes which are used in the tabulation and quantification of the questionnaire are applicable here also. The processes involve counting of frequencies calculation of percentages and averages computation of means, medians and coefficient of correlation etc.

Uses of Checklist

- Useful in gathering facts for educational surveys.
- It is used in observational studies of behaviour.
- It may be used in educational appraisal studies of school, textbooks, instructional procedures, outcomes, school buildings, plans, etc.

Merits

- It systematizes the recording of responses.
- It facilitates the recording of responses

Limitations

- It fails in depth of responses
- It lacks absolute objectivity

Guidelines for Consulting a Checklist

(i) It should be useful in educational research.
(ii) All literature available should be studied before construction of checklist.
(iii) Related items should be grouped together.
(iv) Items are arranged in specific order.

5. Rating scales

Rating is a sample of the reputation of the subject in the eyes of the raters—counsellors, teachers, parents, and others. It is less descriptive and more subjective.

6. Situational tests or behavioural tests

Such tests enable the subjects to reveal some of their personality traits through their reactions, for or against certain contacts with others, and through their spontaneous method of dealing with life situations that confront them, e.g., this individual was used for selecting persons for spying, and other dangerous assignments during World War II.

7. Psychodrama-socio-drama

Role play by the individual, which is spontaneous, in specified situations is observed by trained observers. It is assumed that the individuals project their inner feelings, and conflicts in the role they play.

8. Projective techniques

This enables subjects to project their internal feelings, attitudes, needs, values, or wishes to an external object.

(i) Word association test
(ii) Word connection
(iii) Sentence completion
(iv) Story completion
(v) Rorschach Ink blot test of personality
(vi) Autobiography
(vii) Diary

8

Appraisal in Guidance and Counselling

Nature of Appraisal

It includes comprehensive range of objectives rather than limited subject matter. Modern evaluation uses a variety of techniques of appraisal such as achievement, attitude, personality, and character tests, rating scales, questionnaires, judgement scales of product, interviews, controlled observation techniques, socio-economic method, techniques, and anecdotal records. It includes integrating and interpreting the various indices of behaviour changes so as to construct an inclusive portrait of an individual. For this purpose, comprehensive cumulative records are valuable.

Meaning of Appraisal

1. Evaluation or appraisal is the criteria of success and failure of a task done.
2. Evaluation and appraisal determines the behaviour of students, on one hand, and testifies to the quality of teaching of the teacher, on the other.

Definitions

NCERT defines evaluation as any systematic, continuous process which determines the behaviour of students, on one hand, and testifies to the teaching of the teacher on the other. The paradigms would be as follows:

- The extents to which specified educational objectives previously identified and defined are attained.
- The effectiveness of learning experiences provided in the classroom.
- How well the goals of education are accomplished.

Good defined evaluation is a process of ascertaining or judging the value or amount of something by careful appraisal. And Appraisal is an educational programme which evaluates all the three constituents of the learning process—cognitive, affective, and psychomotor—as well as the end product to arrive at a final conclusion.

Definition of Appraisal from Different Perspectives

Layman—It is value judgement of an individual, or worth of something which is appraised.

Evaluation and Appraisal (value)—These two words should not be used in place of one another.

Schools' and teachers' appraisal means assessment—formative, summative.

Guidance and Counselling—Appraisal is the study of an individual's total personality. This means quantitative as well as qualitative aspects of individual personality.

Curriculum—Evaluation of instructional objectives.

Encyclopedia of education—Appraisal is similar to evaluation.

Dictionary Meaning—A judgement of value, performance, or nature of subject. Appraisal means assessing the weakness and strengths of an individual.

For educationists, appraisal involves the measurement of educational outcomes. It involves both testing of individuals and groups. Its importance in educational practices is widely recognized.

Characteristics of Appraisal

1. *A Comprehensive Process*: All the three domains of human behaviour—cognitive, affective, and psychomotor—can be accurately measured by evaluation apart from students' behaviour, teachers' behaviour (the task of teaching is also evaluated).
2. *A Systematic Process*: It is a systematic and planned process. It is conducted keeping in mind objectives, changes occurred in students and teachers behaviour can be ascertained through appraisal.
3. *Continuous Process*: It is a continuous process of teaching and learning; it goes together with teaching to assess the outcomes of these processes. A list of student's behavioural outcomes is prepared for proper appraisal.
4. *A Social Process*: Whether the expectation of students and society is fullfilled or not is evaluated through appraisal so it is also a social process.

5. *An information collection process*: Appraisal is a broad process which collects information related to student's physical, social mental, emotional aspects. It also collects information related to student's family, interest, ability, aspirations, personality and adjustment, etc.
6. *Combined Process*: It is a combined process which includes the efforts of teachers, parents, counsellors, guidance workers, friends, neighbours etc. for assessing student's different aspects.
7. *A Process of Value Judgement*: This process compares a student's personality aspects to other student's personality aspects which helps in systematic appraised and value judgement.
8. *Appraisal includes measurements*: Appraisal reports may vary from culture to culture. It includes different processes of assessment, evaluation test and examination. It is a comprehensive process which includes measurement in itself. It contains different systems of evaluation like working system, grading system and all sorts of evaluation from practical to theory, internal to external examination etc.

Appraisal reports may vary from culture to culture. Evaluation includes daily observation in the classroom, classroom written work, standardized test scores, and diagnostic tests.

As we guide pupils towards the achievement of classroom objectives, diagnoses of their learning difficulties is needed to determine their readiness for new learning experiences, place them in classroom groups for special activities, assist them with their problems of adjustment, and prepare reports of pupils' progress for parents, we cannot escape making evaluative judgements.

Evaluation = quantitative description of pupils (measurement) + value judgement

Appraisal = qualitative description of pupils (non-measurement) + value judgement.

Evaluation is used as a collective term for those appraisal methods which do not depend on measurement.

Uses of Appraisal

1. *Reporting pupil's progress to parents*—it provides a comprehensive picture of the pupil's progress and development, which provides the foundation for the most effective cooperation between parents and teachers.

2. *Use in guidance and counselling*—Appraisal is useful in guidance and counselling. In fact, the process of guidance is not completed without appraisal.
   a. It assists and provides knowledge regarding abilities, interests, attitudes, and other personal characteristics.
   b. Assist pupils with educational and vocational decision, guiding them in the selection of curricular and extra-curricular activities.
   c. Help people to solve their adjustment problems.
   d. Provide comprehensive picture of pupils' strength and weaknesses in various areas.
3. *Use in school administration*—Used to appraise the special programmes in the school. Administrative decisions regarding placement, grouping, and promotions of people.

Overview

Appraisal involves measurement testing, evaluation, and assessment.

Appraisal in guidance and counselling—Appraisal is an indispensable tool for the teacher. It is not merely a collection of techniques—appraisal is a process. It is a continuous process which underlines all good teaching and learning. Appraisal is inevitable in teaching guidance and counselling.

Quillen and Hanna presented a more extensive characterization.

1. Appraisal includes all the means of collecting evidence on students' behaviour.
2. Appraisal is more concerned with the growth which the student has made than with her/his status in the group
3. Evaluation or appraisal is a continuous process and an integral part of all teaching and learning. It is quantitative as well as qualitative. It is concerned with total quality of personality. It is cooperative effect involving students, teachers and parents.

Why Appraisal is Useful

- It helps in gaining useful information assisting the clients to solve their problems. No test should be given, unless there is some need or justification of it.
- Test results should be shown or given to individuals because we assure that tests are a means of helping individuals to understand themselves. Students need to know their potential ability in order to clarify their own understanding.

- Results should be given in descriptive manner—above average, below average.

How does Appraisal Benefit the Counsellees?

1. How their patterns of interests compare with the pattern of interest of successful workers in given vocations.
2. It helps in determining whether the students are working to capacity.
3. Helps in identifying their area of special interest. A discovery of special ability might give the students incentive and motivation to pursue a previously unknown area of work successfully.
4. Delineates what has been achieved in the school system and what their leading skills are. This helps in discussing the pupils' present and future growth in terms of plans and career.
5. Identifies whether there are any gross variations in the individual's personality traits from those of peers. This helps in understanding their problem of understanding, and their problem of adjustment. Such tests are useful in building case studies of individuals.
6. Appraisal should function as a dynamic technique suitable to the individual in particular situations for the purpose of aiding her/him to develop self-understanding. Finally, by this means it serves its purpose fully in guidance programmes.
7. Maps scholastic aptitude, determination, and application of teachers' instructions accordingly.
8. It helps students to meet their special needs and development as a well-rounded individual.
9. Discovers exceptionally bright and slow learner pupils, so that special provision may be made for remedial programmes.
10. Evaluates methods and techniques of teaching.
11. Provides basis for motivation.
12. Increases the effectiveness of the learning process and improves teacher-student relationship.

1. *Physical Factor*

- Speech
- Hearing
- Vision
- General body condition—motor coordination, growth

2. *Health Factors*

- Eating habits
- Sleeping habits
- Personal hygiene

3. *Psychological Factors*

- Personality adjustment, b. social competence, c. aggressive/submissive, d. attitudes, e. group relations on a person to person basis.
- Aptitudes: 1. Scholastic, 2. Specific
- Interest
- Reading skills
- Mental Health.

4. *Educational Factors*

- Area of superiority/weakness
- Suitability of curriculum
- Co-curricular participation—activity chosen, success/failure
- Suitability of industrial material/methods
- Study and work habits
- Teacher-student relationship
- Student-school relationship

5. *Environmental Factors*

A. Family background:
   - Cultural and social characteristics and influences
   - Attitude towards child, school, society
   - Economic/social status
   - Type of Family, which includes whether a child is brought up through broken homes, single parent or nuclear or joint family
   - Home duties/responsibilities

B. Neighbourhood factors
   - Geographical factors—location etc.
   - Recreation facilities
   - Employment (full/part time)

Need for Appraisal in Guidance and Counselling

An evaluation of pupil potentialities and progress is made through the utilization of standardized tests.

Test and inventories are tools of appraisal by which plans and decisions may be made realistically and intelligently.

The aim of guidance and counselling is better understanding of each pupil. Knowledge about his/her aptitudes, interests, achievements, and personality characteristics contribute to this understanding.

An adequate system of pupil appraisal is essential in gaining needed information.

1. To determine pupil achievement level and progress.
2. To gain data for diagnostic purposes.
3. To ascertain aptitudes.
4. Appraisal is needed to provide for the identification of interests.
5. To improve instruction—The teacher should be better informed about utilization of test data to progress towards superior teaching. Appraisal is needed to determine existing self-concept and attitudes. This can be ascertained through observation, and specific testing instruments.
6. Appraisal is needed to ascertain social adjustment.
7. To identify underachievers and overachievers.

Limitations of testing while appraising students for guidance and counselling:

1. Low motivation of some pupils.
2. Relative narrowness of the traits measured—this statement is made as a precaution, not as a criticism of testing instruments.
3. Low validity and reliability of test for some pupils.
4. The unavailability of local norms—there are sometime differences in norms, which could impact test manual due to local norms being different from those of where the test was designed.
5. When more weightage is given to verbal expressions and vocabulary then it is difficult to score well by those students who lack linguistic or verbal ability, students with low verbal ability find it difficult to understand the instructions given in test and also they are unable to express themselves properly so it is difficult to conduct proper evaluation of such students. In such cases, non verbal performances tests are better options.
6. Failure to follow directions or instructions given in the test.
7. Undue influences of environmental conditions upon test results.

Different Concepts related to Appraisal

Evaluation—It is a new concept in education. This term was introduced to designate a more comprehensive concept of measurement than is implied in conventional tests and examinations.

S. No.	*Measurement*	*Evaluation*
1.	It measures single aspects of subjects, like achievement and specific skills. It measures only quantitative progress of the pupil. It has a narrower aspect.	Emphasis in evaluation is upon broad personality changes, and major objectives of the educational programme. It includes not only achievement, but also attitudes, interest, ideals, values, ways of thinking, work habits, personal, and social adaptability. It measures qualitative progress of behavioural changes also, and has a broader aspect.
2.	It is quantitative in nature.	It is both qualitative and quantitative in nature.
3.	Measurement is a part of evaluation.	Evaluation is continuous process in education and guidance.
4.	It does not involve holistic aspect, but only measures specific aspects.	It always aims at improving the situations as whole in the school.
5.	It only gives measure of any performance.	Basis of remedial teaching is evaluation not measurement.
6.	It is less reliable, valid, and objective.	It is more reliable, valid, and objective.
7.	It covers only cognitive aspects.	It covers three domains of human behaviour—cognitive, affective, and psychomotor.

Assessment—This term is reserved for application to people. It includes the use of testing procedures e.g., Student's achievement in a particular course may be assessed, or student's attitude towards particular aspects of their schooling may be assessed.

All assessments include the use of test results or responses to attitude scales and questionnaires. Two common types of assessment are formative and summative.

Measurement—In guidance and counselling, measurement includes ability tests, typically used to measure characteristics such as intelligence, achievements etc. It is used to learn how much material is remembered or forgotten.

Appraisal is broad. How it can be delimited?

Following are the rules and guidelines meant to delimit and regulate appraisal and evaluation activities.

1. Determine the broad or general goals of the programme.
2. Classify and define goals or objectives in behavioural terms—how many objectives are achieved in behavioural terms.
3. Find situations in which achievement of objectives will be set.
4. Develop and select appraisal techniques as standardized tests and questionnaires, and non-standardized methods.
5. Determine by measuring whether the objectives have been achieved.

Standardized Techniques of Appraisal

Important information for the study of individual:

1. *General Data*—Name, date of birth, sex, birth place, address, etc.
2. *Physical data*—Health of individual.
3. *Family and social environment*—Type of family, socio-economic status etc.
4. *Mental abilities*—Intelligence, I.Q. level for different kinds of jobs
5. *Educational and other achievement*—Subjects, interests, marks, sports and co-curricular activities.
6. *Interests*—Standardized techniques should be used to identify interests.
7. *Aptitudes*—They are inherited and natural, not acquired from the environment. Only standardized techniques should be used to get knowledge about these abilities.
8. *Information regarding adjustment*—Personal adjustment with teachers, friends, parents, relatives. Active participation in different activities in schools.

9. *Record of class work*—It is necessary to know the difficulties a child faced in school for proper guidance.
10. *Knowledge about future plans*—Clash between choice of parents and child for future subject planning, or jobs give rise to feelings of frustration. Therefore, counsellor requires questionnaire and interviews.

Test and Scales Used for Appraisal

Bhatia's Battery of Performance, Koh's and Alexander's test of intelligence.

1. Prayag Mehta's group intelligence test
2. Jalota's group test of mental ability.
3. Asthana's adjustment inventory.
4. WAIS—Wechsler Adult Intelligence Test Scale
5. Kuder's preference records.
6. Strong's vocational interest inventory.
7. Cattell's 16 personality factor (P.F.) test.
8. Cattell's Intelligence Scale (culture fare).

Evaluation Methods

Testing procedures:

1. Oral and written test
2. *Informal test*—teacher made, and specialist made
3. *Subjective*—essay type, and objective test.
4. Mastery test (knowledge skill).
5. Survey test (general achievement).
6. Diagnostic test which reveals disabilities in achievement.
7. Specific content based tests.
8. Individual intelligence test.
9. Group intelligence test.
10. Performance test (verbal).
11. Non-verbal test.
12. Speed and power test (time).
13. Clerical ability test.

Non-Standardized Tools and Techniques of Guidance

(Self-reporting Techniques)

Interview, questionnaire.

Observational Technique

1. Anecdotal records
2. Checklist
3. Rating scales
4. Sociometric techniques to measure social relationships
5. Guess who

Strang—A guidance worker should have knowledge of non-standardized tests along with standardized ones.

1. Questionnaire
2. Anecdotal records
3. Autobiography
4. Rating scales
5. Case study
6. Sociometry
7. Observation
8. Cumulative records
9. Interview
10. Checklist.

9
Guidance for Child Development

Children progress in several areas such as in physical growth, language acquisition, comprehension, or in skills of interaction. Children need to move in order to master body control. They need to explore, manipulate objects, and repeat actions to exercise their mental, social, and manual skills, with enough opportunities to handle materials, experience the world around them, and perform tasks of increasing complexity. Children get their growth needs enhanced through play.

In the formative years between birth and age six, children must be in an environment that enhances their major domains of growth—physical, motor, comprehension, and communication skills. Their environment must give them enough impetus and challenge. This is done by providing them adequate experiences with objects, in interactions, and by enabling them to indulge in activities which appeal to their basic playful nature.

Teach Children How to Learn

Modern thinking on education affirms that the goal of teaching learning process is to teach children "how to learn"; that is, to explore, discover, and practice thinking skills, and process information so as to understand the world around them. According to Rabindranath Tagore, The Principle of True Teaching is that nothing can be taught, and that the teacher is a helper and guide. He/she does not impart knowledge, but helps students to acquire knowledge on their own.

The needs, abilities, and interests of children are in direct relation to age, the patterns of interaction, activities that will foster development in all domains, and the diverse social and cultural practices, concerns, and values that influence children's development.

The child's development can be thought of in different domains or aspects. These are all intimately interrelated and interdependent to interact with each other, so that it may be often difficult to separate them. Yet it is important to do so, lest any domain is neglected, and curriculum should be planned to attend to all domains to achieve holistic development.

Development in each domain can be fostered by giving each child a chance to participate in a wide variety of play-based activities. These activities allow the child to engage actively in the process, to learn, practice, and master skills at each level, to test and evaluate, and to develop self-confidence and motivation to achieve.

The different skills which can be developed through play are to share which develops social and emotional skills, copy a visual pattern which develops visual or sensory skills, and visualize the object which develops their cognitive and imaginative skills.

It is imperative for guidance workers, parents, and teachers to understand children's needs, abilities, and interests at every age and stage of development by observing their behaviour.

Teachers must remember that guidance works as parents and young children learn best in small groups, because it eliminates long waiting periods and offers more person to person opportunities. Young children's attention or any concentrated efforts have a limited span of time.

Suggestions to teachers and parents for encouraging children:

1. Introduce only one or two concepts at a time.
2. Keep games simple, and make sure that instructions are clear. Try to demonstrate as much as possible, especially when introducing a new game.
3. Ensure that each child has an opportunity to participate, and to succeed.
4. Watch for restlessness, and stop when the interest wanes.
5. Do not insist that every child participates in every game. Gently encourage them to take part. Recognize and reinforce a child's individuality.
6. Play games without winners or losers.
7. Give each child a special task, such as being a leader or initiator in order to foster positive qualities.
8. Praise and reward children for cooperative actions, and helpfulness.
9. Create situations where cooperative behaviour is needed.
10. Continue to let children experience the joy of doing, and achieving mastery in their own time.

Physical Development

Children need clean surroundings, plenty of fresh air, play, and exercise for healthy physical growth and development. To develop large and small muscles, children need to practice exercise, such as running, jumping, crawling, skipping, and balancing which makes their bodies strong and skillful in different ways.

Development which is orderly, and progressive, results in changes that are long lasting. Physical development follows two directions—one is the 'head-to-toe' direction, i.e., starting from the head and going downwards.

The second direction that the physical development follows is from the 'center of the body to the ends' that is, development proceeds outwards. The body parts and muscles near the axis (the spinal cord and the trunk) develop earlier, while the parts that are farthest (the arms, the legs, the fingers and the toes) are the last to develop. It is because of this that children use the muscles of their shoulder before they are able to use the muscles of the fingers. Similarly, children are able to control the movement of their legs before they can use their toes. Therefore, children can do gross motor activities using the arms and legs much before they can do tiny activity with their fingers or toes. So, there should be a progression in the activities planned for physical development.

Sometimes, it is best to encourage, under adult supervision, free play. Free play gives children opportunities during the day to run, jump, and dance while playing on their own or with other children. Young children are characteristically very energetic, and cannot sit still for several hours. So, one should ensure that there is plenty of physical movement in their play. The main objective being to help them loosen up and feel comfortable, and develop their muscles.

Children should experience as sense of achievement growing out of their increasing height and weight. Children must develop motor skills—large or gross, motor or muscle control, and coordination of their legs and hands.

Free play, although good, is not enough. Children also need to play organized games in groups. It is important for them to learn and follow the rules of the game, play together, while developing physical motor skills. There must be a balance between free play and organized games.

Children learn about the world around them by using their senses. While playing, they see, hear, touch, move, taste, and smell. This sensory experience and discrimination forms the basis for the development of concepts.

Visual impressions are one of the most important and valuable sources of learning for young children. They learn to experience and name the different colours, shapes, sizes, and patterns that they see, not only in the natural world but in material objects too. Learning to discriminate shapes and patterns, for example, is an essential preparation for learning to read and write.

Sounds are important to children. So, interest in sounds, the capacity to listen, and to discriminate sounds contribute to the development of speech. Children discover many sounds on their own as they explore materials, but they must be helped to identify and listen to individual sounds.

Children are responsive to the feel of things. They learn from touching and feeling, and need a wide variety of experiences with touching in order to develop adequate understanding of the world around them.

Children can identify good and bad taste. But they must be encouraged to use appropriate terms such as sweet, sour, bitter, salty, etc. to differentiate the variety of tastes in the food they eat every day.

There are many kinds of pleasant and unpleasant smells in the child's immediate environment e.g. smell of food, soaps, flowers, clothes, etc. Describing smells increases children's ability to express their perceptions, and to describe their experiences.

The sense of bodily movement is also one of the senses that forms the experience on which the child's learning is based.

Unstructured play, structured activities, and exploration with a variety of objects and sensations are important in the early development of sensory motor skills. Children learn by interacting with concrete or real objects, and the people who are part of their environment.

This is important not only for the development of all the sensory and motor skills, but also for maintaining a high level of interest in their learning. In playing with clay, beads, or construction blocks, they learn to gain control over hand and finger movements, to practice eye-hand coordination, and experience the joy of mastery over objects and materials in the world.

Thinking Skills or Mental Activities

The basic processes of thinking or cognitive skills are the gradual development of the following abilities:

- To discriminate through the five senses, sight, hearing, touch, smell, and taste
- To recognize and match similar things
- To identify, name, and match objects
- To arrange in order along any one dimension

- To observe, remember, and recall
- To classify on the basis of concepts or dimensions, e.g., shape or colour
- To repeat a pattern or to make a logical sequence, e.g., games of repeating patterns, or recalling events and stories in correct sequence, and
- To solve problems and reason, e.g., solving puzzles and mazes.

According to Piaget, the development of thinking ability in all children progresses through four stages. The timing and pace at which they move through these stages may vary from child to child.

Stage of Cognitive Development	*Age*	*Characteristics*
Sensory-motor	0-2 Years	In this stage, thinking is based on sensory input and bodily motion.
Pre-operational	2-7 Years	now children develop symbolic thinking and language.
Concrete operational	5-7 Years	Children use heuristic language
Formal operational	7-11 Years	Next, children deal with logical process, using the simple forms of classification and with the help of concrete objects

Children can develop these abilities earlier and faster if the tasks are simple, clues are given, and all distractions removed. It is also in these years that children learn many new concepts, from everyday happenings, and things they see around them. Understanding abstract concepts of number, time, and space is difficult for young children. A complete understanding of these concepts develops only during middle childhood years.

In organizing play activities to develop these abilities and skills, one must know that some of these activities can be conducted for only one child at a time. Most activities can be carried out either in small groups of three to five children; or in medium size groups, of ten to twelve children. There are also games that can be played by the whole group. Some of these games need no equipment at all, others need a few simple articles. It is worthwhile to make a collection of objects, which can be used for such play activities, especially for children to count, match, classify, and arrange.

Social and Personal Development

Social and personal development includes the development of good habits and behaviour, the right attitudes, and sound values. Social development refers to relations with others, learning how to get along with others, learning to help, cooperate, and live together, to lead, to follow, and learn socially acceptable habits and rules of behaviour etc.; while personal development refers to the growth of self-awareness, self-reliance, self-control, and self-confidence in the child.

During this period, children adopt habits, attitudes, behavioural patterns, and values from their environment. That is why it is important to teach them good habits and healthy attitudes.

The stage in personal development or development of the self can be seen from various angles like:

- Self-awareness in the domain of thinking.
- Self-reliance in the domain of habits, actions, and skills.
- Self-confidence, and
- Self-control in the domain of feelings and emotions.

The best reward for a young child is approval, praise, encouragement, and love.

Don'ts

- Praise the same children all the time;
- Draw comparisons between children;
- Offer bribes such as sweets;
- Make promises that you cannot keep;
- Strike or hit or slap a child;
- Shame a child in front of others;
- Complain to parents about the child's behaviour.

The most humiliating punishment is disapproval, reprimand, or lack of love. This too can be shown in many ways. Keep in mind that punishment must be determined by the age of the child. A young child cannot always understand our reasons for punishment, so the same mistake committed by children of different ages must be treated differently.

As children grow and mature, their emotions proceed through a series of stages, from the infant's relatively undifferentiated responses to what is termed as emotional maturity. By the age of three months, an infant can differentiate between distress and delight. By two years of age, a child can express a full range of emotions, including fear, distrust, anger, jealousy, distress, delight, elation, and affection.

Learning to Express their Feelings

In the early childhood years, children learn new and socially acceptable ways of expressing their feelings. They have to be helped to:

- Recognize and name their feelings.
- Understand and accept them, and
- Find wholesome outlets.

Hostile feelings, aggression, resentment, and other negative feelings are often experienced by children, and have to be recognized and handled. Here are some common situations in which resentment is felt by children and ways of dealing with it.

Feelings of jealousy or hostility arise with the arrival in the home of a new baby. This may show up in school in behaviour such as hitting, and hurting other children.

Children also use verbal aggression against other children as well as adults. When the teacher is aware of this, and provides a warm, supportive relationship, the child will be able to handle such feelings, and even check them.

Another source of resentment in children is the demand made on them to 'keep clean', and the fear and guilt they feel when they get dirty while at play.

Often children, who are very timid or shy, may not show their resentment or hostility openly, but express themselves by doing something quietly, because parents and teachers approve of quiet children. The teacher can help such children by allowing them to express their behaviour.

Failure to get attention and response will arouse resentment and hostility, especially in insecure children, who want reassurance. As teachers, you need to understand that all children need equal attention. When you give attention to one child, others may feel left out.

Teach Them How to Deal with Feelings

Children love to work with their hands. As they do so, they are exploring with their senses, gaining new experiences, using their imagination, practising skills with their hands and fingers, while coordinating, and controlling their muscles. At the same time, they are also expressing their feelings of wonder, joy, and love of beauty, fun, excitement, love, humour, and energy. Children also get great satisfaction, a sense of achievement, and pride in making things by themselves and in communicating their feelings non-verbally through these products. Side by side, they are learning to appreciate beauty of form, both in nature and in man-made things, and in the things that they make.

Performing arts like mime, movement, role-play, song, dance, and drama are constructive ways to channelize and express emotions and feelings, and to communicate. The joys of being able to do what one observes around him/her, and also what others are doing brings a feeling of self-confidence. Acting out troubled situations and real-life problems gives them an outlet for their emotions, and enables them to cope with situations which they may not be able to talk about. Therefore, any material or activity that allows for success, that challenges but does not frustrate, and leaves children with a sense of accomplishment, helps them to express their feelings and acquire mastery over themselves.

Artistic activities also help children express and overcome destructive impulses and negative feelings of fear, anger, aggression, hurt, sadness, and loneliness in ways which do not hurt one or others. Stories, drama, doll play, and role-play give opportunities to enact feelings like fear, sorrow, and anger as well as joy, love, and enthusiasm. They also learn to communicate their feelings, thoughts, and ideas.

Children enlarge their experiences by using their imagination.

Academic Readiness

Academic readiness, or school readiness, as it is often called, is the state when young children are ready to begin learning the three formal skills of reading, writing, and arithmetic. Every child may arrive at this stage at a different age, and at his/her own pace.

Signs of readiness for learning can be seen in children's behaviour, and an obvious interest in an activity, e.g. when a child shows interest in books, she is ready to read. Disinterest in a learning activity may be sign of lack of readiness. Insisting on the activity when children are not interested, whatever may be the reason for it, is likely to produce little or no learning, and may cause frustrations and bad feelings. This may also turn the children against that particular task. Sustained attention also depends upon the degree of interest and curiosity shown by the children, and this can be aroused through play, which is the young child's way of learning.

The principle of readiness does not necessarily mean that you must simply wait for the child to give signs of readiness to learn. Readiness itself can be taught, through many structured and unstructured activities.

The key to foster children's readiness to learn is to provide many opportunities, and a large variety of concrete objects for spontaneous exploration, in a secure trusting climate, extending gradually into more structured learning activities.

Readiness for Reading

Many people believe that reading involves knowing the letters of that alphabet, how to put them together to read words, and how to string words together to read sentences. Sometimes, these skills can be developed and yet the child is unable to read. For reading is essentially the process of acquiring meaning from the printed word. A child may recognize all the words, but may not understand what she reads. So, the real aim of pre-reading is to show that meaning can be derived from what is read, and to enjoy the process.

Children have to be prepared to read with understanding and activities like sorting, matching, classifying, understanding relationships, perceiving patterns, and problem-solving described in earlier chapters, to help the child to achieve the mental maturity needed to relate symbols to sounds and meaning.

Children also need to have fine visual and auditory discrimination, and be able to recognize minute difference in shapes, sizes, and in sounds. While these skills too need some maturity, they can be developed by practice.

Another important factor in learning to read with meaning is mastery over the spoken language. Children who have a good vocabulary, and express themselves freely and clearly, are likely to be better readers. Again, children who are familiar with books, and to whom stories have been read from books are more curious about the printed word, and more likely to understand that printed words hold meaning, and can be a source of fun.

The most significant ways to promote reading are:

- Provide a rich background of stimulating experiences and activities
- Develop children's speech and vocabulary
- Create the desire to read in children
- Give practice in visual, aural, and oral discrimination.

Readiness for Writing

Readiness for writing can be seen in the child's ability to hold a pencil correctly with the fingers, and manipulate it to make the fine movements needed to write. This too is related to maturity, but can be developed by pre-writing tasks, or readiness activities for writing. Some exercises that provide practice in pre-writing skills are:

- Colouring pictures with large crayons
- Colouring or tracing or drawing within lines
- Cutting paper with a pair of scissors
- Threading beads on a needle or string
- Stacking small wooden blocks one on top of the other
- Fitting constructional toys together
- Finger tracing in the air, then on a sand tray, or slate
- Throwing and catching a balloon, a ball, a beanbag, or a rubber ring
- Air tracing with the whole arm, then the wrist, and the pointed index finger while the elbow is firmly placed on the table.
- Scribbling from left to right.

Readiness for Arithmetic

Readiness for arithmetic is shown in the level of understanding of concepts related to quantity, volume, space, time, etc. and in logical thinking in children, which is derived from their mathematical discoveries. At the age of two or three, children know that one block on top of another makes two. They know that if they add one more, they will have three, even though they may not know the words two or three. With each of these experiences, children encounter, and discover mathematical concepts.

- Block building introduces size relationships, number, quantity, and the concept of three dimensionality.
- Dancing allows children to explore and understand space through their bodies.
- Collage and construction activities provide experiences in sorting and classifying.
- Clean up time provides opportunities for comparing, sorting, counting, and arranging.
- Distributing plates, cups, flowers, crayons or pencils to other children teaches one-to-one correspondence, or counting.

These and other concrete experiences are critical in helping children acquire mathematical concepts and vocabulary. Ordering, sorting, classifying, sequencing, seriating, and experiencing one to one correspondence help lay the foundation for mathematical concepts.

In this way, it can be concluded that all round development of the child's personality is a cooperative effort of parents, teachers, guidance workers, and counsellors. Each and every individual responsible should be sufficiently vigilant. Children's needs are different during different stages of growing up. They should be dealt very carefully with a sound background of physical, social, emotional, and economical environment for the concerned child. If psychological principles are kept in mind while dealing with adolescence, it always gives good results.

10

Guidance for Exceptional Children

Gifted, Backwards, Underachievers, and Dull

With growing awareness of the difficulties faced by exceptional children in the ordinary classroom, increasing attention has to be paid towards the guidance and education of such children. They are children, who though different from so called normal children, are often deprived of the special attention and education they deserve and are sometimes even ignored.

These children do not conform to the established norms of society. Catering to the needs of the exceptional children, therefore, contributes to the welfare of all. Education and guidance of exceptional children require the exercise of skills from many fields. Efforts towards integrated teaching have resulted from new efforts.

1. Gifted Children

The gifted children have no abnormality, and they are as well-adjusted and balanced as the normal. In fact, if the conditions in the home, school, and community are always conducive to optimum development, gifted children would develop normally and would make satisfactory adjustment. All physical, emotional, and social needs should be met, if the child is to develop a balanced personality. It is to remember here that gifted children possess some or the other special ability that needs to be nurtured. "When satisfaction is denied, these children may resort to undesirable ways of meeting their needs—ways that set them apart from their fellows" (Strange, 1954). This can turn the child into an eccentric, immature, and emotionally unstable child.

Characteristics

When compared to children of their chronological age, the gifted children are physically stronger, socially more secure, and emotionally more stable. They are more alert, more responsive, and more eager to learn, are better readers, and are more critical of their educational offerings, or the curriculum available to them. They are problematic in classroom when their abilities remain unchallenged or unsatisfied. For instance, gifted children can perform their work in lesser time than other children and may not be able to sit idle in the class after completing their assignments and may not disturb others.

Gifted children are above average in personality traits, scholastic achievements, play, information, and versatility of interests. Their I.Q. is more than 140, i.e. genius.

The following characteristics have been disclosed in the researches of Terman (1930), Witty (1953), and Goodenough (1956). They have better home environment as gifted children are taller, heavier, and better developed. Their parents have had much schooling, have a high intelligence, their homes have culturally, and intellectually stimulating facilities. They prefer games which require reasoning and judgement, and are favoured by children older than themselves.

Gifted children learn to walk and talk earlier than the average children, use a larger vocabulary, and their general language development is faster. They retain information well, and can concentrate for longer periods. They learn to read even before entering school. They develop their reasoning ability early, so, they perceive relationships with insight. All gifted children may not have all these qualities but they vary in their specific qualities.

Guidance to gifted children involves chiefly assistance with a view to meeting their needs, developing their potential, and special abilities, while providing them sufficient and independent information about everything.

What is the Need to Give Guidance to Gifted Students?

1. Gifted students, because of general advanced maturity, are able to utilize counselling at earlier stages than other children. They are able to verbalize, and analyze their problems more easily than other children of the same age. They are ready for self-appraisal, and self-conceptualization at higher levels, or at an earlier age than their schoolmates.
2. Although this advancement may lead to earlier vocational choices, the teacher/counsellor should be cautious about accepting specific occupation choices at an early age. The gifted children may have greater realization of their abilities and interests, but they may not be familiar with all the potential choices open to them.
3. A problem arises in several gifted or talented students because

of lack of orientation or motivation for higher education. This happens more particularly in the case of students from lower economic status. In such cases, abilities must be developed and trained, if they are to be maximally used.

4. There is a problem of underachievement in gifted students. Yet the extent of the problem is not clearly known. However, the reason may be because of a highly developed intellectual ability. They are not interested or attracted towards the class work teaching given in school at that level.

Guidance and Educational Programme for Gifted Children

1. A challenging and rewarding curriculum has to be provided to them after studying their educational and vocational interests and needs.
2. Havinghurst (1955) is of the opinion that a successful educational programme for gifted children would be one that aims at the development of a variety of talents like:
   (a) General intellectual ability, reasoning, verbal skills, mathematical skills, and spatial imagination.
   (b) Ability in science, mathematics, social leadership, and human relations.
   (c) Talent in creating arts, music, creative writing, and dramatics.

He suggested that three general procedures whereby a school can stimulate gifted children, and help them to develop their abilities could be enrichment (primarily a teaching procedure), special grouping, and accelerations (primarily administrative devices).

Enrichment in its productive form means not adding more of the same kind of content and activity to the programme, but providing a greater variety of experience at a more advanced level. Such a programme may be characterized by:

1. Emphasis on creative or the experimental learning.
2. Emphasis on skills investigation.
3. High standard of accomplishment.
4. Individual attention by the teacher to student.
5. Extensive reading.

In special grouping, the gifted children are identified and grouped together, they are provided with activities which are conducive for their full development. Whereas in acceleration the students with gifted ability be given earlier promotions to the higher class.

Strang (1954) in a symposium said that to be prepared for their responsibility in the education of gifted children, teachers need to understand:

1. Who the gifted children are and how to identify them early?
2. How they are influenced by contemporary culture, and other environmental influences?
3. What their characteristics are?
4. What kind of education can best meet their needs?
5. What are issues and problems in the education of the gifted children?

Terman and Oden stressed the importance of:

1. Segregation in special classes.
2. Parallel classes for fast, medium, and slow learners.
3. Acceleration (earlier promotion to next classes).

Parents should provide such environment and guidance to their gifted child, as would help in the adjustment at home, and in society.

2. Slow Learning Children

Slow learner is not a diagnostic category, it is a term people use to describe a student who has the ability to learn necessary academic skills but at rate lower than the average of same peer group.

Sometimes backward children are also slow learners, and may be divided into those with an I.Q. between 76-89, who are educable or trainable; and morons, imbeciles, and idiots whose I.Q. is less than 76. The morons require special education, the imbeciles are untrainable to a large extent, and need to be placed in schools for the mentally deficient, while the idiot can neither be educated nor trained, and have to be institutionalized.

It is the slow learners who come to school, because they constitute a fairly large (about 15%) segment of the school population, and are capable of only poor quality, slow, and limited school achievement.

Skinner (1904) states their characteristics as:

1. Limited capacity to deal with abstract things. Limited ability to discriminate numerals, sounds and numbers.
2. Inferior reasoning in practical situations.

3. Inability to interrelate several situations.
4. Need for greater supervision.
5. Need for more external stimulation and encouragement.
6. Inferior understanding of rules or conduct in games and social situations.
7. Low school achievement. Poor memory.
8. Slow speed. Poor reading and writing ability.
9. Inability to keep pace with classmates.

Guidance Programme

1. Their instruction has to be made as nearly functional as possible. Some slow learners can be trained in semi-skilled trades. Their educational development can be promoted in schools that provide ability grouping, and separate classes.
2. Schools and parents must see that these children are not unnecessarily discouraged.
3. As slow learners have limited span of attention and concentration, they must be provided repeatedly those fundamental things which are necessary like reading, writing, and arithmetic. They should be given experiences from which they will learn about the nature of the culture in which they live, and how to get along in society.
4. The goals set for them should, therefore, be attainable, with more opportunities for success, and frequent praise, rather than discouragement.
5. When learning in the classroom becomes difficult for them, they often cause issues of indiscipline. So, the teacher should teach keeping their needs in mind.
6. Some children, who are emotionally disturbed, are also not able to learn, even when they have an I.Q. similar to their group. Their problem should be tackled professionally.

3. Dull

Generally, people fail to distinguish between a backward and dull child. Backward children are those who have a normal brain, but for certain reasons do not progress like other children of the school, and remain backward. In a backward child although the number of nerves cells and fibers remain normal, yet they do not develop to the extent they ought to. The backwardness could be due to social and economic reasons.

The dull children are those who are inferior in intellect to children with normal brain, but are better off than the feeble-minded children.

The cause of dull intellect is a shortage of nerve cells relating to higher intellectual activities in the body. As the result of this shortage, the mental development is slow and the child lacks in efficiency and character. The child is not capable of learning any subject. Generally, this defect is born with child and it is difficult to get rid of the deficiency. The I.Q. of such children is between 70 and 85 as compared to a normal child, i.e. their I.Q. is 15 to 30 less than that of a normal child.

Symptoms—Such children start speaking and walking late. Their teeth also come out late. They have a lethargic and dull expression on their faces. They walk lazily, and lack concentration or reasoning power. Their characteristics are as follows:

1. They find difficulty in abstract situations. So, they deal only with concrete situations.
2. It is difficult for them to establish cause and affect relationships. They have difficulty in planning and decision making.
3. They have problems of adjustment as they are more rigid.
4. They lack imagination and visualization.
5. They make friends mostly below their age level.

Guidance Programmes for Dull Children

Education and guidance programmes for dull children—Particular attention should be paid towards the studies of dull children. The moment suspicion arises about their dullness; they should immediately be shown to doctors.

1. *Individualized methods of interactions*—Children with extremely dull minds are not suitable for ordinary school teaching. There is a need for individualized teaching, instructions in separate schools.

2. *Special education institutions with remedial teaching*—Such schools should be opened for them, where fresh air and sunshine is in abundance. There should be big fields where they may play freely. Personal attention and remedial teaching is necessary in case of children with dull minds.

3. *Counselling service*—It should be provided to them when they act like immature children.

4. *Vocational guidance*—These children should be provided with practical vocational guidance to face the difficulties in life. Their education should be so patterned that more physical work is involved in it. For example, they should be taught gardening, carpentry, leather work, book binding, tailoring. For the girls of this category, arrangements should be

made for learning tailoring, weaving, cooking, washing, etc. They should be given more opportunity for physical exercises, sports, and dance, etc. They should be asked to clean the house, wash the clothes, polish the shoes, and perform other household work in order to create a feeling of responsibility in them.

4. Underachievers

Low achievers are those who do not perform even with normal I.Q. level. So, their achievements are also very low. Underachievers are those who are not able to achieve according to their I.Q. They may also be gifted, but even having high I.Q. they are not able to achieve up to the mark.

High achievers are those who achieve more than their I.Q.

Causes and remedies to improve achievement have been suggested by different psychologists. Not just gifted students are underachievers; the more or less backward students may also present a problem in underachievement. As in the case of the gifted underachievers, the discrepancy between potential and achievement may be related to a number of factors. For example they may not be attracted or motivated to doing their class work. So, they do not achieve accordingly.

1. Some studies stressed specified abilities such as reading, which gives origin to underachievement. Emphasis was placed on programmes of remedial work and training in methods of study has also been used to remedy defects in study habits and development of skills.
2. The importance of the emotional factors in underachievement is being increasingly recognized. Students may fail, or achieve below their potential, because of the presence of personal and emotional problems. This suggests that the therapeutic counselling or psychotherapy may be effective in helping underachievers. Group therapy has been reported as effective in improving achievement.
3. Some studies have shown that mothers of high achievers were found to be more authoritarian and restrictive than mothers of low achievers.
4. It is interesting to note that the selection of students who were underachievers show the lacking adjustment power also.
5. Underachievement is a problem with a variety of causes ranging from inadequate previous preparation or instructions, through deliberate efforts not to achieve at a high level because of fear

of being considered a grind or an egghead and preoccupation with family problems, to emotional disturbances and lack of recognition of potential. Poor or inadequate background or preparation may be remedied by special instruction or tutoring. Other causes are matters for counselling rather than instruction. More and better counselling services in our schools would indubitably lead to the reduction of underachievement, and more efficient utilization of the talents of students. Some other factors may also lead to underachievement, like socioeconomic factors and social pressure. These cannot be remedied by counselling, because these may always be individuals who may choose not to achieve up to their potentials in the academic area, because they prefer to concentrate their efforts on something else for social recognition.

11

Education of Exceptional Children

Problems and Measures

"Labeling refers to the act of assigning a child, or a condition to a general category or to a particular position in the classification system."—(Hobbs 1975). By implication, it is generally negative. A label indicates that a stigma is present, particularly with mild handicapping classification, e.g., mental retardation, specific learning disabilities, emotional disturbance. In day to day life, we often use labels for various purposes. Labels exert direct influence on our behaviour towards persons, objects, situations.

Although, anyone can refer a child for special education, it is usually the regular teacher or parent who exercises this responsibility. A regular classroom teacher can use observation, criterion-referenced assessment, and curriculum-based assessment for referral purposes. A teacher can observe systematically and collect baseline data, and develop the criterion referenced test (CRT) to know how well or poorly a child is doing compared to others. Recently, the concept-based assessment (CBA) has received considerable attention. This is an assessment procedure in terms of the expected curricular outcome of the school. The teacher simply monitors the progress with respect to school's curriculum.

There are both positive and negative sides to labelling. Hobbs (1975) stated that labels led to improved legislation, improved communication, and the development of advocacy agencies. On the negative side, there are possibilities of stigmatization, peer rejection, and wrong labelling of minority group children based on inappropriate tests.

Most severely challenged students are identified prior to school age by parents and physicians. The majority of mildly challenged students are usually identified by administration of educational and psychological tests. The physical or sensory disabilities are identified by non-educational procedures. Psychological and educational tests are non-referenced tests to identify mental challenges. These are relevant to most exceptional students. Labels are given according to test scores obtained by the child.

Some of the commonly used tests of intelligence and achievement used in assessing children for labelling purposes are:

1. Wechsler Intelligence Scale for Children—Revised
2. Kaufman Assessment Battery for Children (sequential and simultaneous processing)
3. Wide Range Achievement test—Revised
4. Peabody Individual Achievement test—Revised
5. AAMD Adaptive Behaviours Scale.

The education of exceptional students is largely placed in the hands of the special education teacher. Of course, the regular teacher too takes responsibility, as well as the school counsellor, specialists, and therapists, wherever available. However, once a student has been deemed eligible to receive special education, it is essential to develop an individual education programme (IEP)

Assessing children for identifying handicaps is a necessary step for placement. Assessment in the field of special education has been more controversial than any other area of special education. For effective placement of a child in special education institution, and for mainstreaming, two issues are of special concern:

(i) assessment principles, and (ii) assessment procedures.

Assessment forms an integral part of the process of intervention. Assessment data should dictate intervention, on the one hand, and the nature of the pupil, on the other hand.

1. Usability of the test for purpose other than those for which they were designed e.g., use of intelligence tests for remedial and compensatory intervention, whereas its function is for classification and placement. Intelligence score does not tell the teacher how best to teach. It simply shows the extent to which an individual child differs from others who took the test.
2. Use of technically inadequate tests in decision making and lack of concern for the type of culture to which the child is exposed as well as using inadequately constructed norms as reference points. Diagnostic personnel should not routinely administer such tests to children, or use normative scores to interpret and make important decisions. Careful consideration of the target group is necessary with reference to its cultural background. Measurement instruments must have empirical evidence for their validity and reliability for use in such groups.

3. Use of deficit score to identify handicapped children is very much in vogue in case of learning disabled children. Discrepancy between capabilities (IQ test) and achievement levels are often used to identify the disabled learners.
4. Bias in assessment has been a subject of regular debate. Tests used should not only be non-discriminatory, but decision makers should not be biased while making decisions basing their judgement on race, sex, SES, physical characteristics, parental power, etc. Labelling has a tremendous effect on teacher's expectation, and assessment of cognitive competence and achievement.
5. Assessment of abilities versus skills is another issue. It is better to use skill development models rather than the ability training model for design of instruction of the disabled.
6. Competence of persons who assess the child varies very widely in our country. There is virtually no certification for test users in India.

Deinstitutionalization

Several concepts are used in this field to connote mainstreaming or integration such as deinstitutionalization, normalization, least restrictive environment (LRE). Deinstitutionalization means that removing retarded persons from institutions, and placing them in other environments. Mainstreaming means educating retarded persons as much as possible in classes with non-retarded persons. Integration basically means mainstreaming. Normalization means that the individual's total environment should be as close as possible to that of the non-handicapped person's environment. Segregation is desirable only when the nature of the handicap is such that education in regular classes with the use of supplementary aids and services cannot be achieved satisfactorily.

Deinstitutionalization is a trend which grew in reaction to institutionalization. In institutions, disabled children were considered physically or mentally ill, and received treatment, but no care and education.

Deinstitutionalization includes three processes: (1) reversing institutionalization by finding alternative placement, (2) returning to the community all residents who have developed the skills necessary for successful transition, (3) establishing residential environments that protect rights, and lead to a rapid transition to the community.

Mainstreaming

Over the years, things have improved as diagnosis has become multidisciplinary. Education has become the emphasis, trained professionals are available. Hence, the need for integration and mainstreaming is felt more now. Mainstreaming is an approach that emphasizes integration, and as such it is the antithesis of the earlier institutionalization movement which emphasized segregation.

The council for exceptional children (CBC) has specified the essentials of mainstreaming the mildly disabled.

1. Providing the most appropriate education for each child in the least restrictive environment (LRE).
2. Concentrating on specific educational needs, rather than on labelling.
3. Developing means by which regular classroom personnel can serve students with adjustment problems.

Mainstreaming is the education of mildly handicapped children in the regular classroom. It is a concept that is compatible with the least restrictive environment concept that all the handicapped can be educated with their normal peers whenever possible. It is based on the philosophy of equal educational opportunity, which is implemented through individual planning to promote appropriate learning, achievement and social normalization. (Stephens, Blackhurt, and Magliocia, 1983).

Mainstreaming does not mean placement of all exceptional students in regular classes. The key to mainstreaming is the placement of the mildly retarded in the regular classroom environment that best fits their needs. It can even be a regular classroom for the part of the day. Sometimes, it may not include a regular classroom but is a special class in the regular setting, and extracurricular activities determined by consideration of how best we may promote learning, achievement, and social normalization.

Mainstreaming is a particular orientation towards supplying special education to the majority of the mildly retarded in particular, and the handicapped in general. Environmental stimulation has significant positive effects on the development of retarded children.

While sociometric studies admittedly showed low acceptance by non-handicapped peers of handicapped children in mainstream classes; they also showed that in special classes there is lower academic achievement. A few showed that in a special class, there is lower academic achievement, while some social models have been developed from which the handicapped children could learn interpersonal skills.

The concepts of integration and mainstreaming aim at bridging the differences between milder conditional opportunities under the least restrictive environment. The delivery models of such integration include placement of a mildly disabled child in a regular class with resource teachers for all purposes of acquisition of academic and social skills; an itinerant special teacher plan for a cluster of schools; partial integration where the disabled child lives in a residential setting but attends most of the classes in regular classes of a day school. Special classes are conducted with the children, however, taking part in co-curricular and other activities of the school.

The objectives are to bridge the initial entry differences in:

a. academic achievement,
b. social skills, and
c. economic sufficiency through development of vocational skills within the limits of the special children's educability.

The aim is never to replace special education classes or schools which could meet the demands of the severely disabled/retarded. In a word, the objective of integration and mainstreaming is normalization under the least restrictive environment (LRE).

Mainstreaming has often been interpreted to mean that handicapped students must be instructed in regular classroom settings. According to the U.S. Department of Education (1984), 68 per cent of handicapped students receive most of their education in regular classes in the U.S., while an additional 25 per cent are enrolled in special classes located in the same buildings as regular education classrooms, placement of these classrooms in regular classrooms, or within the school buildings is presumed to give handicapped students more opportunities to be in contact with non-handicapped peers. Such exposure is thought to present behaviour patterns for handicapped students to emulate.

Placing handicapped students in the same classroom as non-handicapped students seems to result is desegregation. These students may occupy the same space, but they may not be engaged in activities with one another. However, placement in regular classroom per se does not result in improved achievement or social status.

Handicapped students' social status has improved when programmes were planned to help integrate them into the regular class setting. Kaufman, Gottieb, Agard and Kukic (1975) and Wang (1981) emphasized this as follows.

1. Mainstreaming refers to the temporal, instructional, and social integration of eligible exceptional children with normal peers. It is based on an ongoing, individually determined educational needs' assessment, requiring classification of responsibility for coordinated planning, and programming, by regular and special education administrative, instructional, and support personnel.
2. "The term mainstreaming is used to mean an integration of regular and exceptional children in a school setting, where all children share the same resources and opportunities for learning on a full-time basis" (Wang, 1981, p. 196).

Integration

Integration is another expression used to mean mainstreaming. Integration cannot be reduced simply to an educational issue, or an employment issue. Its achievement will require the successful coordination of a whole series of transitions for the handicapped, ranging from early identification, to early intervention, to school programmes, to community, jobs, and finally to community living.

An approach to integration that takes the individual needs of the special child into full consideration may result in one or more of the following.

- *Physical integration*—Planning for the location of special programmes in school buildings with regular education programmes.
- *Social integration*—Planning for regular personal interactions between students who have handicaps and those who do not.
- *Academic integration*—Planning to ensure students with and without handicaps use school resources simultaneously.
- *Societal integration*—Planning designed to enable students with moderate and severe handicaps to work, live, and spend leisure time with their fellow non-handicapped students.

***Some ways this can be achieved*:** Providing special services within the regular schools. Supporting regular teachers and administrators. Having students with disabilities follow the same schedule as non-disabled students. Involving disabled students in as many academic classes and extra-curricular activities as possible including music, art, field trips, assemblies, and exercises. Arranging for disabled students to use library, playground, and other facilities at the same time as non-disabled students. Encouraging, and helping in building relationships between disabled and non-disabled students. Arranging for disabled students to receive their education in regular community environments when appropriate. Teaching all children to understand and accept human differences. Enrolling disabled children in the same schools they would attend if they did not have disabilities. Taking parents' concerns seriously. Providing an appropriate individualized programme.

Things which should not be done: Dumping students with disabilities into regular programmes without preparation or support. Locating special education classes in a separate wing at a regular school. Grouping children with a wide range of disabilities and needs in the same programme. Exposing children to unnecessary hazards and risks. Ignoring children's individual needs. Placing too many demands on teachers and administrators. Ignoring parents' concerns. Isolating children with disabilities in regular schools. Putting older students with disabilities in classes for younger children, i.e. age inappropriate placement. Maintaining separate schedules for students in special education and regular education.

How can Mainstreaming and/or Integration be Achieved?

Reynolds, *Education and Training Mentally Retarded,* volumes 17 no. 3 (Oct. 1982) p. 171-176 has suggested a set of specific targets in 10 different areas for effective mainstreaming and/or integration.

1. *Curriculum*—The preparation of all teachers should include the study of, and first-hand experience with curricular principles, guides, and structures from pre-school through secondary school levels. The means and the procedures by which curriculum is developed, adopted, and changed should be understood. There should be practice in designing, and modifying curriculum and materials, especially to suit the individual needs of students.
2. *Teaching Basic Skills*—The preparation of all teachers should include necessary elements to assure competency in teaching the basic skills (defined to include literacy, life-maintenance, and personal development skills).
3. *Class Management*—All teachers should be proficient in class management procedures, including a variety of ecological interventions, group techniques, crisis interventions, etc.
4. *Professional Consultation and Communication*—It is essential now that all teachers have opportunities to master the knowledge and practices involved in effective consultation and other forms of professional communication. All teachers should be skilled at group problem solving.

5. *Teacher-Parent-Student Relationship*—All teachers should have skills and sensitivity while dealing with parents and siblings of handicapped students.
6. *Student-Student Relationships*—All teachers should be able to convey to students, the positive attitudes necessary for productive interactions with normal peers.
7. *Exceptional Conditions*—All prospective teachers should have full knowledge about exceptional children, about school procedures for accommodating children's special needs, and in the functions of specialists who serve exceptional children. Moreover, opportunities for direct experience with the children and with specialists should be provided.
8. *Referral*—Teachers need to learn the procedures for referrals, the responsibilities involved, and the ways to capitalize on referral resources to obtain better education for individual pupils.
9. *Individualised Teaching*—All teachers should be competent in the assessment of the individual student's educational needs, and in adapting instructions to the individual. Teachers should have working knowledge of the IEP development process.
10. *Professional Values*—Professional educators' values ought to reflect a primary emphasis on the needs and rights of individual students.

The following issues emerge from the above for the purpose of implementing the integrated/mainstreamed education scheme:

1. Degree of segregation in the educational setting has to be spelled out for the mildly disabled. What type of integration would best fulfil the objectives needs to be decided.
2. Supportive systems and services for psychological, recreational, and vocational skills development have to be visualized and introduced.
3. Instructional procedures have been stereotyped due to the lack of exposure of existing teachers to special teaching techniques. There is need for in-service as well as pre-service teacher training.
4. Existing negative attitudes of teachers, and normal peers towards mildly disabled children's capacities need to be changed.
5. Parental involvement and community participation in the total scheme of integrated education is important. The parents constitute a vital factor in the child's care and acceptance at home.

6. Integrated schools should use sensory stimulation, and life skill training.
7. Routine placement of a mildly disabled child in regular school without due process of identification and diagnosis, and prescriptive teaching is meaningless.
8. Normal and mildly disabled teacher-pupil ratio, in classes needs major attention.
9. Preparation for early intervention programmes, quality of intervention, and management must be made.
10. Behaviour management resource specialists should be used, and resource rooms installed.
11. Professional intolerance and alienation among specialists of different disciplines should be minimized.
12. Delineation of activities by different service delivery systems in the total scheme of integrated education is required.
13. Development of infrastructure and instructional materials in regional and state languages for the resource room is needed.

Measures in Special Education

Teachers should be managers of learning, facilitators of the learning experience rather than disbursers of information. All teachers need time to work with individual pupils or groups of pupils. Experienced teachers can catch up time of few minutes before recess, during lunch, or after school to help those pupils who need extra instructions. During this time, they also help children to begin homework.

Small Group Instruction

Using small group instruction is another way to make mainstreaming more effective. Before using this technique, the teachers should have sufficiently developed their classroom grouping skills to enable small pupil groups to function smoothly. They should be taught how to work in groups. The following instructions could be as starting point.

- Choose your two most trustworthy pupils.
- Assign them each a specific task to be completed outside class, such as preparing for a science demonstration.
- Excuse the pupils from regular class work. Make the assignment a choice one.
- Compliment pupils for a job well done.
- Get ready for complaints from others for such choice assignments. Now the stage is set.

- Select a reliable pupil and one of the less reliable ones.
- Gradually extend this procedure over five or six weeks to more and more small groups.

Make sure that having a group assignment remains a privilege. This will encourage good behaviour.

Mastery Learning Strategy

Mastery learning techniques offer a systematic way to give pupils longer periods of time to master skills and concepts without penalty. In the long run, mastery learning can save time by reducing the time for revision. Bloom (1964) has found that mastery learning hinges on pupil perseverance and aptitude, and on the clarity of the teachers' instructions. Pupils' perseverance tends to increase as they realize that they are learning.

- Restricting mastery learning to the basic curriculum.
- Beginning with the most essential basic skills.
- Providing pupils with a short list of skills to learn.
- Having each pupil study, practice, self-test, recycle, and retest with final checking (testing) by the teacher until mastery is achieved.
- Initially, allowing about 10 to 15 per cent more time for handicapped children.
- Drawing on assistance of tutors from other grades or the same grade, teacher aides, parent volunteers, programmed instructional units, microcomputer drills.

Mastery learning is an optimistic theory about teaching and learning that many teachers can virtually get all students to learn excellently, swiftly, and self-confidently. Both exceptional and non-exceptional children can benefit from the system of instruction, if it is systematic, if the tasks are broken into small steps, if goals are clearly stated, if sufficient time is given to the learners, and there is some criteria of what constitutes mastery.

Mastery learning programmes are used successfully in special education programmes under IEP. Some of the materials used in special education classes are based on mastery learning principles. In order to make it more effective, a resource room with a resource teacher are required.

Resource Room

The concept of resource room gained popularity following the declaration that the tracking system was illegal. Tracking system is one by which children, based on IQ test achievement, are placed in different classes, according to their ability. The resource room concept is a promising alternative to placement in self-contained classes or regular classes without support services. Usually, students attending resource rooms are mildly handicapped and gifted exceptional children.

A resource room is a class which special needs students attend for less than 50 per cent of their school hours. The resource room is staffed by a resource room teacher. Attendance in the resource room is determined by a multi-disciplinary staff, according to the students' individual needs. Students attend in specific time slots when they receive instruction from a trained specialist in their deficit areas.

A resource room should be well-equipped with a wide variety of instructional material, individualized instruction may include perceptual training, language development, motor training, social and emotional development, and academic skills development. Resource room class size should be small. The recommended size per teacher would be no more than 20 students at any one time. Class sessions are either individual or in small groups of up to five students per session. The sessions should continue for a minimum of 20 minutes, and a maximum of 45 minutes in length. The resource room should have the same comfortable characteristics of a regular classroom, should be at least 150 square feet size with adequate lighting, and ventilation. It should be easily accessible to teachers and students, and possess adequate storage space for folders and materials. In general, the resource room should provide a positive learning environment.

Resource Teacher

A resource teacher's role is open ended and limited only by time, talent, and acceptance of the teacher by the school administration and staff. The resource teacher is a trained specialist who works with, and acts as a consultant to other teachers, providing materials and methods to those who are having difficulties within the regular classroom. Usually, the resource teacher works with the mildly handicapped population in a centralized resource room. The resource teacher should:

(a) Conduct and participate in the screening of children with learning disabilities, determine their learning abilities, and prepare final report for referral.
(b) Provide instruction in small groups and individually.

(c) Prepare lessons for a child who cannot function in a regular classroom.
(d) Provide resource room help till the child is fully integrated in the regular class.
(e) Provide consultation to the regular classroom teacher and parents.

A resource teacher is a highly trained professional who is capable of diagnosing the child, planning and implementing the teaching programme, assisting the classroom teachers, providing continuous evaluation of the child, and conducting in-service sessions with other educators, and the community.

The role of the resource teacher includes direct service to individuals and assessment and delivery of individualized programmes.

The special education/resource room teacher needs to:

- Find out if the student has the skills to function in the classroom.
- Identify the physical or academic adaptations needed for the student to function in the regular class.
- Identify the students' strengths and weaknesses,
- Provide the handicapped student an opportunity to visit the regular education class, and meet the teacher before enrollment.
- Determine the adapted equipment or the special services needed by students to function in the regular class.
- Participate in planning for mainstreaming activities.
- Participate in parent and community orientation programmes on mainstreaming.
- Seek out consultative relationships with specialists on the school staff.
- Develop programmes to prepare special students for entry into regular classes.
- Prepare members of regular classes for the entry of special students into the class.
- Gather information to determine the educational needs of each student.
- Evaluate each student's present level of functioning,
- Determine goals for each student that are appropriate, realistic, and measurable.
- Determine group goals for the class as a whole, and for subsets within the class.
- Involve parents in setting goals for their children.

- Design teaching procedures that provide for individual differences among students.
- Prepare a variety of activities that will involve the entire class in grouping patterns that are varied and flexible.
- Design a variety of alternative teaching strategies.
- Develop plans for using human and material resources.
- Develop a flexible time schedule that provides for learning, as well as the physical and social needs of each student.

Peer Tutoring

Training pupils to teach one another, one to one, or in small groups provides an extensive opportunity for individualized instruction. Peer tutoring is defined here as two, three, and sometimes four or five pupils working together on the same task. Typically, one pupil is being taught by another. Peer tutoring is mutual and interactive. In order to ensure it, the classroom teacher has to work out how to start, monitor, evaluate, and terminate. Peer tutoring has salutary effects.

Programmed Instructions

Programmed instruction is well-suited for individualized instruction and for mastery learning. Programmed instruction can be effective in meeting the needs of several types of exceptional pupils:

- Because the material content has been thoroughly task-analyzed, slow learning pupils experience success.
- Visually impaired pupils can benefit from those programmed materials that have verbal responses using auditory presentation.
- Hearing impaired pupils can benefit from visual response formats.
- Pupils with superior abilities can often experience an enriched curriculum by using programmed material.
- Programmed materials also help pupils, who have health problems, to catch up on content when they have been absent for a period of time.
- Physically handicapped pupils whose upper extremities are affected can benefit from programmed materials that do not require written responses, especially if the machine is easily advanced to the next frame.
- Programmed materials can provide regular classroom teachers with another method of meeting the individual needs of a variety

of pupils. The up-to-date mode for presenting programmed instruction is the microcomputer.

Use of Microcomputer

Microcomputers in the classroom are another very powerful tool for the mainstreaming teacher. The computer is probably the most powerful tool ever developed for helping pupils of widely varying needs, achievement levels, learning problems, or interests. The computer brings teachers extra pairs of quality hands. It is highly motivating to most pupils.

Technology for the Disabled

During the last 15 years things have changed greatly. Silicon chips and microprocessors have changed society. Technology is gradually changing the life of disabled. The computer has two characteristics that have significance and meaning for the disabled—(a) decrease in size of hardware; (b) increase in sophistication to make it easier to use. Micro computers can be attached to wheel chairs to improve mobility. They are more accessible for use by handicapped people, because mere key strokes are needed to perform computer functions.

Physical education programme has three basic functions—(i) input functions, (ii) abilities, (iii) motor skills. Basic input functions include equilibrium reflexes, vestibular system vision, audition, tactile, and kinaesthetic success. Perceptual motor abilities include balance, laterality, directionality, body image, spatial awareness, cross-lateral integration. Physical fitness parameters consist of strength, muscle, and cardiovascular endurance, and flexibility. Motor abilities include speed, power, agility, and motor coordination.

It is necessary, that practitioners, teachers, resource team should have a thorough understanding of the various aspects of disability and processes.

12

Institutions for Exceptional Children

Special education movement in India is of relatively recent origin. However, institutions which have come up for education, care, and rehabilitation during the last two decades in a significant number, if not proportionate to the target clientele, yet are significant enough from near zero base.

Mentally Retarded

Of all the kinds of handicapped people, the mentally retarded constitute the largest segment, but is the most neglected field in India. There are very few institutions of teacher training in India for training teachers of the mentally retarded. Teacher Training in Special Education, Mumbai; B.M. Institute of Mental Health, Ahmedabad; the All India Institute Speech and Hearing; Kamayani School of the Mentally Retarded, Pune; Bal Bihar Training School, Chennai; Alakendu Bodh Niketan, Kolkata; Karnataka Parent Association for MR, Bengaluru; Jai Vakeel School for Children in Need of Special Care, Mumbai; Thakur Hariprasad Institute of Mentally Handicapped, Hyderabad; YMCA, Nizamuddin East, New Delhi; Central Institute of Mental Retardation, Thiruvananthapuram; North Calcutta Pratibandho Seva Kendra, Kolkata; National Institute of Mentally Handicapped, Secunderabad and its regional centres; Banaras Hindu University, Varanasi; Jamia Millia Islamia, New Delhi; S.N.D.T. Women's University, Mumbai; and R.K. Mission Mahavidyalaya, Coimbatore are the institutes/universities who have undertaken the responsibilities of training teachers for mental retardation (MR) in terms of certificate courses; Bachelor in Mental Retardation, Diploma in Special Education; B.Ed. and M.Ed. in Special Education, Post-Graduate Diploma in Mental Retardation. The institutes addressed themselves to offer teacher training for the teachers of mentally retarded students. These institutes also offer one/two-year Diploma in teaching the mentally retarded. The number of students admitted in these institutions are limited, i.e., about 600 in all in these institutions.

The curriculum includes: Education for handicapped children, psycho-educational assessment, methods of teaching mentally retarded people, behaviour therapy, psychology of the handicapped, medical care of the handicapped, occupational therapy, auditory and speech therapy, and project work. At present, curricula have been standardized by RCI.

Visually Handicapped

Till 1980, there were four centres for the training of teachers of the blind or visually impaired, one each in Chennai, Kolkata, Delhi, and Mumbai. Each centre provides specialized training for preparing teachers of the blind. The expenditure is met 100 per cent by the Central Government. The annual intake of these centres is 50 students.

The Regional Training Centre for Teachers of the Blind, Poonamallee, Chennai; Training Institute for Teachers of Blind, Mumbai; National Institute for Visually Handicapped, Dehradun; Ramakrishna Mission Ashram Blind Boys Academy, Kolkata, West Bengal; Regional Training Centre of the Blind, New Delhi; and Alakendu Bodh Niketan, Kolkata are institutions in India which offer teacher training for the teachers of blind people. These courses vary from 60 days' duration (in-service) to one academic year (pre-service), and a diploma is given on successful completion of the course. At present, there are about 15 such teacher training centres where B. Ed., M. Ed., Diploma, and certificates are given.

Recent centres include NIVH, regional centres, and university departments. Some of these are: Blind Relief Association, New Delhi; Divine Light Trust for the Blind, Mumbai; Handicapped Welfare Department, Andhra Pradesh; R.K. Mission Training Centre, South 24-Parganas, West Bengal; NAB, Karnataka; Poona School and Home for the Blind Trust, Pune; R.K. Mission Mahavidyalaya, Coimbatore; Jamia Millia Islamia, New Delhi; Kurukshetra University; Andhra University, Waltair; Mahatma Gandhi Gramyo Yog Viswavidyalaya, Chitrakoot.

The curriculum that is followed in these institutions includes—Educational psychology, principles of education, education of blind and visually impaired, methods of teaching, history of education and rehabilitation of the blind, anatomy and physiology of the eye and eye diseases, and Braille technique.

The curriculum is almost identical in all the training institutions, and each institution offers practical training and practical examinations during the course.

Speech and Hearing Problem

The various training institutes: Government Lady Noyce Secondary

School, Ferozeshah Kotla, New Delhi; School for Deaf and Dumb, New Delhi; Training Institute of Stephen's High School for the Deaf and Aphasics, Mumbai; The Centres for the Teachers of the Deaf, Lucknow; Education and Audiology Institute for Teachers of the Deaf, Mumbai; V.R. Raja Teachers' Institute for the Teachers of Deaf, Pune. The teacher training curricula for the teachers of the deaf currently in vogue provide instructions for a period of one academic year, and award a diploma or certificate which enables the graduates to enter into teaching profession. Clark's School for the Deaf, Chennai; Education Auditory and Research Society, Mumbai; Holy Cross College, Tiruchirappalli; Institute of Speech and Hearing, Mysore; L.L. Institute of the Deaf, Bhavnagar, Gujarat; Little Flower Convent Higher Secondary School for the Deaf, Chennai; V.R. Rina Mook-Badhir Vidyalaya, Pune; Training College for the Teachers of Deaf, Kolkata; Sheila Kothavala Institute for the Deaf, Bengaluru; Central Institute of Teachers of Deaf, Mumbai are the institutes which offer these courses.

There are also graduate and post-graduate courses in about 15 centres in the country. The course content includes: audiology and learning aids, psychology, principles of education and class management, anatomy and physiology, history of education of the deaf, sound, curricular studies, phonetics, methods of teaching, arts and crafts, problems of the deaf. This course provides practice teaching along with practical and theory classes. On an average, 350 teachers are enrolled into the various courses every year.

Orthopedically Handicapped

The Spastic Society of India, New Delhi; Spastic Society of West Bengal, the National Institute of Orthopedically Handicapped, Kolkata; Spastic Society, Mumbai offer short term programmes of teacher training varying from 12 days to 60 days. Courses include: medical and therapeutic aspects of child development, normal psychology, and the psychology of handicapped individuals, and educational aspects of normal and special children.

These short courses are in-service in nature, since no special training for teaching is necessary for teaching the orthopedically handicapped. These courses are very new, and do not have a regular intake, although each one is equipped with adequate trained personnel. The National Institute of the Regional Centres concentrate on short-term teacher training as well as pre-service teacher training programmes.

With the assistance of UNICEF, since 1979-80 courses were

organized for teacher training—one by the Spastic Society of India, and the other by the B.M. Institute for the Teachers of Mentally Retarded Children. Various courses on orthotics, prosthetics, occupational therapy (OT), physical therapy (PT), rehabilitation, developmental therapy etc. are conducted by several institutes such as: Christian Medical College, Vellore, Seth G.S. Medical College, Mumbai; Institute of Social Sciences and Research, Vellore; Patna Medical College; Vikalanga Kendra, Allahabad; School of Prosthetics and Orthotics, Chennai; Dept. of Rehabilitation, Safdarjang; All India Institute of Physical Medicine and Rehabilitation, Mumbai.

The All India Institute of Speech and Hearing, Mysore

This Indian Institute was established in 1965, and is managed by the Government of India. It has exceptionally well qualified staff for imparting therapeutic services as well as teacher training in the areas of mental retardation, deafness, and the orthopaedically handicapped. The graduate degree leading to Bachelor of Science is of three years' duration, and the post-graduate degree leading to M.Sc. is of two years' duration. There are also facilities for advanced research in all these areas of handicap, including speech and hearing disorders leading to Ph.D. The annual intake is more than 23 and 13 for graduate and post-graduate courses respectively. This institute is an ideal one for undertaking research and innovation in special education in the years to come. The institute brings out the Journal on Speech and Hearing.

National Council of Educational Research and Training (NCERT)

The National Council of Educational Research and Training (NCERT) were established on 1st September 1961 with its headquarters at New Delhi with a view to improving school education. It is an autonomous organization registered under the Societies Registration Act, 1860, and functions as the academic adviser to the Ministry of Education and Social Welfare. In formulating and implementing its policies and programmes in the field of school education, the Ministry of Education draws upon the expertise of the NCERT.

With reference to special education, NCERT earlier had a department of special education within teacher education, and special education cells in all its four Regional Colleges of Education. It pioneered the running of six months key/resource teacher training at its headquarters, and multi-category training of Teachers in the four Regional Institutes of Education. Besides, it has assisted in running one week course on teachers' training of primary teachers, six weeks' intensive course for selected teachers of PIED. The Regional Institutes of Education also ran B.Ed. and M.Ed. courses with specialization in one area of special education until recently. These courses are in the process of being phased out. The special education unit is now with the new department on disadvantaged groups.

At the centre, several in-service programmes are also being run for principals of DIET, special education faculty of SCERT/SIE, and PIED block supervisors at various times. The main contribution has been, among others, implementing of PIED project, development of instructional manuals, promotion of research and documentation, preparation of handbooks on hearing impairment, visual impairment, PIED, etc. It has been also responsible for feeding information to database for POA, 1992, and Policy Guidelines NPE, 1986, and NCTE Committee on Special Education as well as to RCI.

NCERT has introduced MCT programme to prepare manpower for meeting the needs of integrated education in schools. The course is run in its four Regional Institutes of Education, and in a few centres e.g., Amarjyoti Trust, New Delhi, and JSS Teacher Training Institute in Bengaluru. The course is of one-year duration, and is not disability specific. About 100 teachers are trained every year. The course structure includes comprehensive coverage for enabling the teachers to develop competency to handle major disabilities.

Guidance workers and counsellors should:

- Develop an awareness that all school teachers, whatever the age group of their pupils, or level of their work, are likely to be concerned with helping some children who have special educational needs.
- Enable teachers to recognize early signs of variable special educational needs.
- Give the knowledge of the part which they can play in the amount of child's educational needs, and in the execution of any special measures prescribed.
- Inform teachers what special education is like, together with the knowledge or range of various forms of special educational provision and of specialist advisory services.
- Provide some acquaintance with the school classes and units.
- Give teachers an understanding of how to communicate effectively with parent's anxieties, and encourage their continued involvement in their child's progress.
- Give teachers in-service training of when, and where to refer

for special help, and knowledge in general terms of teaching them handicapped skills required by teachers.

- Practical skills in observation of children, both individually and in groups, to help teachers sharpen their perception of variations in children's learning and behaviour and develop their awareness of variation in children's circumstances (home/school difficulties).
- Appreciation of the educational needs of children with developed difficulties—physical, sensory, emotional, behavioural, or learning the needs of their parents, and the value of the contribution which parents can make to their children's development.
- Understanding of the practical steps necessary for meeting a child's special needs and an ability to adopt the attitude must suit to dealing with particular difficulties and to appreciate the need for modification of the school or classroom organization, the curriculum, or teaching techniques.
- Appreciation of the special services available to children with special needs of their familiar and of the advisory services available to teachers. This might be developed by inviting professionals for the various services to visit the college, so that through discussion, the students can learn about the work of teachers in relation to other professionals, the contributions which different specialists can make, the services to expect from them, and the kind of questions to put to them.
- Awareness of the range of the career and professional opportunities in special education, and the availability of further qualification in special education, and the fact that special education offers the teachers engaged in it an intellectual challenge.

Rehabilitation Council of India, New Delhi

The aims and objectives of the rehabilitation council are as follows:

1. To regulate the training policies and programmes in the field of rehabilitation of disabled people.
2. To bring about standardization of training courses for professionals dealing with disabled persons.
3. To prescribe minimum standards of education and training for various categories of professionals dealing with disabled persons.
4. To regulate the standards in government institutions, central as

well as state, uniformly throughout the country.

5. To recognize institutions training professionals in the field, recognize the degree/diploma/certificates awarded by these institutions, and to withdraw recognition.
6. To recognize foreign Degree/Diploma/Certificates on reciprocal basis, and to get Indian Degrees/Diploma/Certificates recognized abroad, and to withdraw such recognition.
7. To maintain an Indian Rehabilitation Register.
8. To collect information regularly, on education and training in the field of rehabilitation of disabled persons from institutions in India and Abroad.

The Council has standardized several courses for different categories of manpower requirement in the field of special education.

National Institute for the Mentally Handicapped, Secunderabad

The National Institute for the Mentally Handicapped was established in 1984 as an autonomous body under the Ministry of Welfare, Government of India. The Institute serves as an apex body with specific emphasis on training and research in the field of mental retardation. The NIHM offers specialized services, keeping in view the various requirements of the mentally handicapped persons.

The aim and objectives are:

(a) To develop appropriate models of care and rehabilitation for the mentally retarded persons, appropriate to Indian conditions.
(b) To develop manpower for delivery of services to the mentally handicapped.
(c) To identify, conduct, and coordinate research in the area of mental retardation.
(d) To provide consultancy services to voluntary organizations in the domain of mental handicap, and to assist them, wherever necessary.
(e) To serve as a documentation and information centre in the domain of mental retardation.
(f) To acquire relevant data to assess the magnitude causes, rural-urban composition, socio-economic factors etc. of mental retardation in the country.
(g) To promote and stimulate growth of various kind of quality services for persons with mental retardation throughout the country.

At the Institute's headquarter at Secunderabad, there are six departments, namely, medical sciences, psychology, special education, speech pathology and audiology, information and documentation services and vocational training. The Institute has three regional training centres located at Mumbai, Kolkata, and New Delhi, while the Model School for the Mentally Deficient Children at New Delhi was taken over by the Institute in 1986. Some of the Institute's training programmes are also carried out by a network of supported and affiliated centres spread across the country.

The National Institute runs the following pre-service, in-service, seminar, and other training programmes:

(a) Three years Bachelor's Degree Course in Mental Retardation (BMR) at Secunderabad.
(b) Diploma Course in Mental Retardation.
(c) Post Graduate Diploma in Mental Retardation.

The Institute organizes 10 to 12 short term courses every year. The duration of such courses is three to five days. The courses cover: (a) portage programme, (b) vocational training, (c) behaviour modification, (d) appreciation programme for AIR producers, (e) media workshop on disability.

Each year, a national level seminar on mental retardation is organized by the Institute which serves as a platform to professionals working in the field of mental retardation to exchange information, including parent training programmes.

The Institute provides multi-disciplinary team services for helping the mentally handicapped persons and their parents. Usually, all the cases that come to NIMH are assessed by a general service team for psychological, clinical, and educational assessments. After identifying the different requirements of the mentally handicapped individuals, and their families, intervention, and programmes are decided which include appropriate referrals, further remediation in special services of the institute, and providing consultancy to organizations such as special schools. The services available include: behaviour modification, early intervention for preschool children, group activities, medical management, parent/family guidance and counselling, physiotherapy, special education intervention, vocational training and guidance, psychosocial services.

Karavalamban Kendra

This special education centre located at NIMH headquarters at

Secunderabad admits about 85 children with mental retardation in the age range of 3 to 16 years. Children are grouped into pre-primary, primary, secondary, and pre-vocational levels. Admission is offered for a period of two years to children with mental retardation, who have been regularly attending the group activity training programme of the Institute. This special education centre also runs group activities for children with mental retardation during the afternoon hours. About 250 children per week benefit from this programme. The children in the morning school programme as well as in the group activity programme are provided systematic training, and can participate in extra-curricular activities which include music, dance, drama, sports, and other recreational activities. Special programmes such as special Olympics are also actively organized. Parents and family interaction during all programmes is encouraged.

The institute has 12 family cottages which offer stay and training facilities in its campus at Secunderabad. Parents who come from far off places, and like to spend time with expert staff at NIMH find the facility of such a service extremely useful.

The Model School was established in Delhi in 1964 by the Government of India, and later transferred to NIMH in 1986. About 110 children—both boys and girls in the age range from 5 to 18 years—are currently on their roll. Around 40 children stay in the residential hostel. There are 12 classes at various levels of pre-primary, primary, secondary, pre-vocational, and vocational. Apart from regular school programme of training in skills, extra-curricular activities like sports, music, drama, and recreational activities are encouraged.

Early intervention services are offered by the NIMH Regional Training Centre (North), Delhi for very young children with delayed development, and mental retardation up to five years of age. Every month about 40 to 50 children benefit from this programme. The parents are given instructions for home management programme after demonstration of the skill training activities at the centre by the trained staff.

In 1992, the vocational training centre was established which offers services of vocational training to persons with mental retardation above the age of 16 years.

To reach people living in remote areas, the Institute periodically conducts rural camps. The activities include: (a) screening and case detection, (b) individual assessment and counselling, (c) training of parents, (d) creation of awareness, and (e) reference.

In collaboration with NCERT and Central Institute of Educational Technology, the Institute has produced programmes which are regularly telecast as a part of the school TV programmes on Doordarshan every alternate Saturday. This programme is directed towards parents having children with mental retardation, and provides instructions for home management of children. This programme is telecast in different languages.

National Institute for the Visually Handicapped, Dehradun

The National Institute for the Visually Handicapped (NIVH), Dehradun was established in July 1979, after amalgamation of the National Centre for the Blind. The latter was started in January 1950 with a training centre for the adult blind, taken over from St. Dunstan's Hostel for the Indian war blinded. Subsequently, other units such as a women's wing, a workshop for making Braille appliances, a sheltered workshop, a central Braille press, schools for blind and partially sighted children, and a national library for the blind were added.

The basic objectives of the Institute are:

- To promote research;
- To undertake the training of personnel; and
- To provide certain national level services.

The National Institute for Visually Handicapped is a registered society under the Ministry of Social and Women's Welfare. Its director is the executive head. The Institute has the following divisions: (i) School Division; (ii) Training Division, (iii) Aids and Appliances Divisions; (iv) Research Division; (v) Book Division and (vi) Industrial Psychology Division.

The activities of the institute include operating schools for the blind, imparting occupational training, running of a sheltered workshop, a Braille press, a teacher's training centre, and conducting research on several aspects of blindness.

The institute operates two schools—one each for the blind and for the partially sighted children. These schools prepare the blind children for the secondary examination. It is the task of these two schools to try out new methods of teaching and equipment.

Model School for the Visually Handicapped

The School provides education to the Blind and partially seeing children till secondary level. Both types of children are given education through media compatible with the nature of their limitations. Blind children are taught through Braille, while partially sighted children make use of magnifying devices to read print. The children are provided free boarding, lodging, clothing, tuition, and other facilities besides monthly pocket money.

The school is affiliated to the Central Board of Secondary Education for its IXth and Xth Class. The School has opened a pre-school unit.

Ali Yavar Jung National Institute for the Hearing Handicapped, Mumbai (AYJNIHH)

The National Institute for the hearing handicapped has been set up in Mumbai. The foundation stone was laid on 25 December 1978. The Institute has been functioning since 1981. It has its regional centres in the country.

There is also a training centre for adult deaf which was established in 1962 at Hyderabad, and has continued to provide occupational training to deaf boys and girls in the area of sheet metal works, fitting, carpentry, electric wiring, cutting and tailoring, welding, photography, turning etc. These students are drawn from all over the country. Recently, the institute has made further studies by expanding education and training activities with latest audiological equipments to provide service facilities. Research programmes include early identification of hearing impairment. The courses run by AYJNIHH are: D.Ed. (Deaf), B.Ed. (Deaf), B.Sc. (AST), D.C.D.

Thakur Hariprasad Institute of Research and Rehabilitation of the Mentally Handicapped, Hyderabad

Thakur Hariprasad Institute of Research and Rehabilitation for the Mentally Handicapped was established in 1968. It offers:

1. Special education programmes tailored to meet each student's special needs.
2. Modern home like residential foster care mother settings.
3. Health care services.
4. Transitional services from school to work and other programmes.
5. Extensive vocational and rehabilitation programmes.
6. Therapeutic recreational activities.
7. Special programmes for children and young with autism and behavioural programmes.

It has made significant contribution in the field of MR in India over the last decade.

13

Research and Innovations in Domain of Exceptional Children

Research and developmental activities in the education of exceptional children have emerged in recent years as areas of concern for researchers. Whatever research has been done in different areas of disability are more of an organizational and institutional nature. It is, therefore, a piecemeal academic exercise neither reflecting a view-point based on our socio-cultural ethos, nor leading to any viable practical application. Excepting biomedical researchers in mental retardation, researches have predominantly been in the areas of attention, learning, and memory, but often dealing with tasks that have less relevance in the classroom setting. A few researches cover the ground in the domain of applied behaviour analysis and behaviour modification.

Researches in the area of speech and language disability are rather more rigorous, but are confined to a particular institute and more in the line therapeutic frame. Research, in the true sense, has not reached an appreciable degree of acceptance as far as assessment of educability and remediation programmes are concerned in the area of visual, auditory, and orthopaedic impairments.

There are various constraints responsible for such a backdrop. Lack of trained personnel, lack of institutional support, late recognition of the idea that disabled children within the mild or educable range can be trained, and several other socio-cultural constraints have allowed little progress on this front. This situation has slightly changed, but is not very conducive to extensive and intensive studies and developmental activities in the area, primarily because of lack of organized effort by the specialists in the respective areas of disability.

It is, therefore, against this backdrop we must plan our research which will provide continuity and comprehensive data based understanding of the process in which the disabled child can gainfully be helped to learn within the limits of their educability, feasibility, and practical application. Especially it will also be able to give a picture of educational level research wherever the approach is normative, and at institutional and individual levels where the need is specific. Keeping these broad goals and background, a perspective of research has been given with some hints of research areas and topics of interest in general.

Problem Issues

Although in the working group report for the education of the disabled some nine categories of disabilities have been identified for care, training, and education in a phased manner, according to the magnitude of incidence; yet there is a need for status studies relating to incidence, service institutions, education and training institutions, in terms of physical facilities and resource specialists in each area of disability, and their major classification and referral practices in vogue. The major thrust in this section should be an understanding of the psycho-educational characteristics of the disabled (i.e., the cognitive, affective, socio-emotional, information processing nature, physical, and motor activities, perceptual style, etc.) on a normative basis against which deviance can be identified and categorized. Such norms are of primary importance for placement of children in a special category, and managing special services for them. At present, such norms are conspicuously absent in our literature. Another area of concern is the content analysis of school curriculum in each of the major categories of disabled in vogue in our country with a view to developing a uniform curriculum. The existing disparities are so great that no one system will be adequate for all categories of disabled children, who are currently receiving education and training in different institutions, voluntary, or governmental.

Such is the case of teacher training curriculum of the disabled. Recently, the special education unit in the NCERT has analyzed the course content, and has arrived at a common teacher training curriculum in the areas of visually handicapped, hearing handicapped, mental retardation, orthopaedically handicapped with a composite course structure. However, the viability of these attempts needs to be examined in relation to objectives of training. The Rehabilitation Council of India has also standardized the curriculum for as many as 34 courses in the domain of disability.

Since language disability has not been spelt out presently as a separate area of disability, one cannot deny that language is the medicine for any cognitive, affective, or skill learning that takes place. Language deficit is one of the major deficiencies in the disabled. The differential communicative competence, and language competence should be studied through development of a Language Assessment Kit for the disabled, which will eventually help in developing language intervention programmes for different groups of disabled children.

Special Instructional Strategies

Curriculum and instructional procedures can be clubbed as one major areas of research concern in the domain of disabled. More specifically, reading readiness programmes need to be developed first, for each area of disability and level within a given disability area. The existing curricula for normal children need to be watered down to the level of the disabled child. Only curriculum research could take such a step regarding arithmetic, reading, language, social skills, etc., to determine empirically the efficacy of a specific method of teaching these curricula. We should develop disability specific instructional technique through research. Such researches are necessary because the western studies prescribe so many varieties of teaching approach and aids that one really needs to know which one is more effective than others. Systematic and coordinated research work have been a felt need because ours is not an affluent country, but a growing and developing one. To make the design of curricula, and methods of instruction effective for the disabled, research in these areas is imperative.

Conducive Educational Environment

Disability is often caused by environmental factors, and more so precipitated by the environment in which one lives. This brings into focus the place of a disabled child in home, in school, and in society. The home also has different variations like the delivery systems in school, and in community. A child who is disabled is perceived and managed in a poor home differently than if he/she is born in a well-to-do home. What is more important in this context, therefore, is the prevailing attitudes, stereotypes, prejudices, and expectations about the disabled.

Before any systematic intervention or educational programme is undertaken, it is necessary to assess the pre-existing status in this regard, or else even the best programme is not going to make any difference. Same is true of classroom climate and management of peer attitudes for a better adjustment. Hence, it is necessary to assess attitudes through research, bring changes in attitudes for better adjustment through intervention, develop such material for dissemination, disseminate the right kind of information about the disabled among people and parents.

All these aim to provide the disabled the least restrictive environment conducive for their optimal growth, and adjustment to living.

The relative merits of isolation and mainstreaming would be another research direction to examine the long-term impact that the disabled have upon society and family.

Biomedical research is imperative to identify and prevent parental influences accounting for incidence of disability, and the biochemical screening after birth, dietary habits, etc. that would go a long way in reducing its occurrence in society. Western countries have come up with many answers of which several are universal, but others are culture specific, e.g., an expectant mother and women in general in India do not smoke or drink, do not expose themselves to too much of radiation. However, there may be other factors like malnutrition, ignorance about infectious diseases, etc. which could have an ante-natal impact on the child. Hence, investigation would be necessary in this regard to identify culture specific influences which act as predispositions for causing disability slowly, but surely.

Research Strategy

Disability is a complex phenomenon. It has multi dimensions and multi causality. Hence, while pursuing any systematic research in this area, there is a need for collaborative effort among institutions, individuals having expertise in the specific areas of concern for any fruitful result, and development of the disabled.

Research strategy may take both cross-sectional, and longitudinal studies approach. We may rely more on clinical case studies and observation, but certainly normative studies are necessary. But, no matter what method or strategy we follow, our aim should be to understand casual, evaluative, and functional variables in the education and training of the disabled, with focus on studies on post-school adjustment in family and society, which are the ultimate goals of any education and rehabilitation programme. Thus, research in this area would provide not only a continuity in thinking, consistency in results, but will prepare a sound empirical base in the domain of special education which mass media can use for the benefit of all, and more so, for the disabled.

Research Developments in Special Education

It is true that recent years have noticed a change from medical diagnosis to multi professional assessment, treatment to education, categorization to individualized needs programme, Category specific needs (Evans and

Verma, 1990; Pandey and Advani, 1995), yet research in India has not made much headway in the field of special education. Perspectives for education of the disabled has been provided by Narsimhan and Mukerjee (1986), research (Panda, 1974) rehabilitation but most of what is available in psycho-educational research on disability are quite limited. A glance at the *Indian Journal of Mental Retardation, Disability and Impairment*, and the *Journal of the Institute of Speech and Hearing* would substantiate such observations, although except for disability and impairment, the other two are virtually out of scene.

Quite a few significant studies have appeared under the guidance and involvement of individual researchers, by and large, rather than of institutes. Noted amongst them are the contributions of Prof. A.K. Sen and Prof. (Mrs.) A. Sen at Delhi University with reference to mental retardation, and specifically on learning and memory processes (Das, 1968; Goel and Sen, 1985), psychosocial integration of the handicapped (Sen, A., 1983, 1988), (Prof. K.C. Panda), on response cost and positive reinforcement (Myreddi, 1995), peer modelling (Narayan, 1992), self-injurious behaviour (Peshwaria, 1993), community attitudes (Panda, B., 1992), integrated education of orthopaedically handicapped (Rath, 1993), reading comprehension of the deaf (Sahoo, 1995), personality structure of the blind (Khan, 1990), isolation effect on learning (Panda, P. 1995), etc. are among the significant ones. NIMH has also researched into skill development in Mental Retardation.

The areas of disability which have received much attention at the doctoral level research are mental retardation, visual impairment, gifted individuals, hearing handicapped, and learning disabled during the last decade. However, the number of researchers is very few, and quality wise is only contributing to understanding the disabled.

Researches have concentrated more on learning, memory, attention, personality, community attitudes, and efficacy of systems, but have hardly ever oriented towards interventions, barring those which aimed at skill development, and development of learning packages. National institutes, NCERT, and university departments have not catered to significant research, but contributed more to education and training of personnel for handling the disabled. Efficacy studies have come up recently (Mani 1993; Rath 1993) but researches taken as a whole in the field of special education are still few and far between.

There is no denying the fact that even now, the domain of disability is regarded as an area of welfare, rehabilitation, and care rather than research, development, and education. Both the directions are important, and research can well integrate the two to the advantages of the disabled.

Areas of research could systematically include: assessment test/checklist development in each area of disability; its regional translation and adaptation; standardization of functional behaviour checklists, even conditions of adaptation from western countries; measurement of change of progress in disabled children as a result of training, ecological intervention, parental involvement, and establishment of cultural norms for clinical as well as research use; prevalence of disability, its incidence in rural-urban set up, incidence rate, socio-demographic antecedents and consequences.

Research endeavours must specify comparative studies on different therapeutic interventions and practices, the role of sensory stimulations early in the process of development, and identify efficient procedures for developmental quotient, and not merely IQ changes, competence, skills, and social personal adjustment which would be the primary focus leading to school readiness. Such research areas are painstaking and challenging, but worth undertaking.

Special education in our country is an emerging field, but there are many sound research generalizations in places where the field had an earlier origin. It is time for us to think, and decide based on our own studies whether home based interventions are any way better than the institution based interventions, integrated system vs. the specialized system, efficacy of community based rehabilitation, and family studies. Public attitudes, acceptance, and awareness are to be assessed and manipulated through various awareness programmes since how disability is perceived at home is influenced by the negative attitudes and stigma of the society.

Technology has come a big way. How can it be used to the advantage of the disabled in terms of aids and appliances, classroom learning, teaching, self-learning, and mastery learning? The role of evaluation which diagnostic as well as normative, microprocessors, and their use to teach the disabled must be reviewed. Many such issues will appear. These are only some directions. While disability specific research is a matter of individual concern, these are some of the areas that come in any area of disability.

Methodology of Research in Special Education

Behavioural scientists tend to be obsessed by their methods, often at the expense of their results. It is not proper to enter into any philosophical debate on the process, nor can any methodological formula for scientific research be defined. The principal way of ensuring competence is to do it and develop insight. These methodological issues relate to designs in research, sampling frame, and to size qualitative vs. quantitative research techniques. The field of special education is essentially fraught with many such issues, since researchers in special education have migrated from other disciplines with their well established rigid, hard core, or soft-core training, and temperament. The field of special education can still follow a clinical model, a sample size of 1, a single subject research design using withdrawal or multiple base line data; across behaviours, across subjects, across situations, without sacrificing research ethics, propriety and rigour. Quasi-experimental design can take care of extreme groups in such research, as purposive sampling is an acceptable practice in spite of procedural lapses and regression, when sample size is not large as is typical in the field of special education.

What is needed is that researchers in special education should take care of the methodological issues even when they use qualitative research techniques for fact finding, participant observation, interviewing, documentation, and review. The fact should remain that it should maintain credibility, transferability, dependability, confirmability, authenticity, and fairness.

It is difficult at this stage to speculate and think of research on disability from a futuristic angle; yet it is a part of programme building and research planning process. Research in future, and particularly in 21st century, will be more concerned with avoidance of discriminatory practices and maintenance of human rights, so that disabled children have full participation in society. Hence, community research will understand our priorities, not just through legislative activism. But this is an open direction. What is more crucial for this group is that disability is more often accompanied by mental problems. Hence, research in mental health, psychiatric social work, and psychological interventions are, and should be, points of reference in planning research activities.

Research in the next decade should focus on the development of functional skills, even using computer technology, and computer aided instructions.

(a) Allow students to proceed at a more individual pace, thereby reducing stigmas.
(b) Enable developmentally disabled to work at home.
(c) Provide learning aids specifically designed for a group of disability.

Suggestions for Future Research Areas

(a) Identification of available services and resources.
(b) Development of learning potential assessment device test as a basis of diagnosis.
(c) Epidemiological investigation of the disabled population.
(d) Research and advocacy of treatment approaches and techniques.
(e) Community integration with a comprehensive care system and a full operational prevention process.
(f) Identification of individually suitable teaching practices, peer tutoring, modelling, education, and service delivery system.
(g) Family studies.

These are but a few suggestions. There will be many more, if we are genuinely committed to the cause of helping disabled children in our society.

14
Mental Health and Adjustment

Mental Health

Mental Health refers to the principles of mental hygiene and their implication for effective adjustment. Mental hygiene based practices at home, school, and in the community that contribute towards the development of healthier and integrated person.

The World Health Organization (WHO) identified four aspects of an individual's total health, viz., physical, mental, social, and spiritual. It refers to the all-round well-being of a person. Mental health is nothing but absence of any mental illness or a negation of any mental trouble.

However, the concept of mental health extends a little beyond this layman's concept the important *characteristics of mental health* are:

1. Personal adequacy
2. Harmonious living
3. Social effectiveness

Thus, mental health is a happy blending of intellectual, emotional, physical, social, and spiritual qualities that a person is endowed with.

Mental Hygiene

It is a science which deals with the measures to reduce the incidence of mental illness, by prevention, and early cure of mental disorder.

Scope—Mental Hygiene, in a broad sense, is the art of helping people to achieve fuller, happier, and more effective lives with the advancement of the medical science. People have learnt to take precautions against diseases such as small pox, tuberculosis etc. Similarly, with the change of the attitude towards mental illness, the idea of prevention of mental disorders dawned on the mind of progressive people.

Mental Hygiene in a stricter sense is the art of preventing mental disorder by applying the theories of the psychology of adjustment. The American Psychiatric Association defines mental hygiene as measures to reduce the incidence of mental illness through prevention and early treatment, and to promote mental health. Essentially, mental hygiene is an educational programme with two fundamental objectives:

1. The fostering of an objective and sympathetic attitude towards the mentally ill.
2. The prevention of mental disorders by healthy psychological living, and the early treatment of minor disorder.

Attitude towards Mental Patients

The mental hygiene movement aims, on the one hand, at creating in the minds of people an attitude of understanding and sympathy towards the mentally ill, and a realistic way of looking upon mental illness, on the other. The counsellors in their professional capacity have many opportunities to dispel misconceptions regarding mental illness, and to stress the right way of thinking in the matter. 80 per cent mental disease is curable and only 9.2 per cent mental diseases are inherited and incurable.

Prevention of Mental Disorders through Healthy Psychological Living and Self-Improvement

Principles for the prevention of psychological disorders in children and adults:

(i) *Prevention of psychological disorders in children*—In 1930, the first International Congress of Mental Hygiene was held in Washington D.C. in which several countries participated. The movement passed through several stages, to arrive at the conclusion that the environment in which children grow up has much to do with their psychological problems.

(ii) *Creation of child guidance centers or clinics*—In this they listen to child's problems and correlate it with parents' attitude and teachers attitudes and then treatment is provided.

(iii) *Prevention of psychological disorders in adults*—To be well-adjusted implies the maintenance of harmony between the demands of one's nature, and those of one's environment. Self-control is the key to living a civilized life, and a key to inner culture. One should know how to keep stress and anxiety at a tolerable level.

The following things are necessary conditions of mental health.

1. *Self-understanding*—That means that besides arriving at an objective estimate of one's abilities and interests, weaknesses

and strengths, a person must try to understand why she/he feels shy, inferior to others, and ill at ease in the presence of superiors, or why not take proper care of positive aspects of is her/his personality. This is self-understanding.

2. *Self-acceptance*—Under different situations, it is both an effect and a condition of mental health. It implies the formation of realistic self-concept which includes one's strengths and weaknesses. It makes people live comfortably with themselves. They accept a realistic approach to life situations, and are neither overly elated in success, nor dismally discouraged in failure.
3. *Acceptance of others*—It flows from a warm understanding of others. The persons, who accept others, do not reject, hate, or dislike others when their behaviour or values are seen to be in contradiction to their own standards or values. Rather they accept others have the right to their own beliefs, values, attitudes, and standards.

Talk over your problems with someone you trust. It promotes interaction between both of you, thus stimulating a constructive attitude in you. Self-improvement is not achieved by what a friend tells you to do, but by what you yourself do. Other factors like a feeling of self-reliance, and of achievement etc. are also responsible for inculcating a sense of self-improvement.

Mental Adjustment—Three Criteria

1. **Related to Self**
   (a) Self-knowledge
   (b) Self-acceptance
   (c) Self-control
   (d) Integration of psycho-physical system of personality
   (e) Socially acceptable habits
   (f) Adaptability.
2. **Affecting Others**
   (a) Sense of responsibility
   (b) Social maturity of response
   (c) Social consciousness—values, norms.
3. **Related to Personal Growth**
   (a) Wide range of satisfying experiences
   (b) Attitude towards reality
   (c) Well-defined goals
   (d) Trying one's best to achieve goals.

Counselling and Adjustment

Adjustment is the process by which a living organism maintains a balance between the needs, and circumstances that influence the satisfaction of these needs.

Human Adjustment

Adjustment—The concept of adjustment originated from the biological term adaptation. We know that the history of evolution of humans is the history of adaptation to the climatic conditions. Both nature and the world at large make demands or create problems for individuals who need to deal with them. You must understand that these problems are never ending. In our society, we must abide rules and regulations. If we deviate from the social norms, we have to pay penalty for it. Of course, society rewards us when our activities are beneficial for it.

Individuals try to maintain balanced and harmonious relationship between their own needs (inner environment), and demands of the society (outer environment). This is a continuous process by which an individual strives to cope with his/her inner needs, tensions, frustrations, and conflicts.

Thus, adjustment is the psychological process by which an individual manages or copes with various demands.

Characteristics of Adjustment

1. *Adjustment is subjective*—Since no two individuals are alike, their coping processes cannot be similar. Besides, inner and outer demands, tolerance for frustration, attentiveness, and adaptability, ability to profit from experiences, values, prejudices, attitudes, and social norms make the adjustment a subjective process which is known to only the person who is adjusting.
2. *Adjustment is a continuous process*—Adjustment is not a once for all affair. It is a process which continues through dealing with stress and strain in life. Hence, a person considered to be quite adjusted now, may have severe adjustment problems, or even total adjustment failure at some other time in an exceedingly stressful situation.
3. *Adjustment varies from culture to culture*—A person considered well-adjusted in one society with a particular cultural background, may not be considered so in a different society with a different cultural setting e.g. an undressed male in a particular sect of a religion or half-dressed men or women of tribal cultures

may not be considered as adjusted in other societies with different cultural backgrounds.

Maladjustment

Determinants of Maladjustment

College and university students face adjustment issues as they are passing through a period of growth. Problems may result in feelings of inferiority, emotional immaturity, identity crisis, excessive concern with body health, etc.

1. Emotional strain due to the process of higher education.
2. Somatization, obsessive rumination, and sexual conflicts are due to poor life adjustment in their previous history of physical or psychological illness.
3. The community to which the students live also contributes to the behaviour problems like lying, stealing, obscene speech, and excessive sexual interest.
4. Defective home discipline, broken homes and disproportionate punishment given by parents is also responsible to a great extent for the feeling of insecurity in students.
5. Some mental causes are also responsible for the maladjustment, like when some students cut classes or manage proxies, as they find the environment dull and monotonous. Poor achievement of student is highly correlated with the incidence of maladjustment.
6. Lack of adequate and positive outlets for youthful energies leads to anti-social activities.
7. Financial problems sometimes lead to low achievement, and lower adjustment.
8. Lack of facilities of guidance and counselling are also potent causes of student's problems. This could be due to lack of effective communications between the faculty and students.

Symptoms of Maladjustment

1. *Physical*—Sometimes an adjustment problem arises when an individual is physically challenged and the people around him are not supporting or helping him in running his life smoothly. This generally happens to individuals who are handicapped due to mishappening in later stages of life instead of by birth.
2. *Behavioural*—Similarly behavioural problems also leads to

maladjustment. The root cause of these problems is sometimes within individual or sometimes in his environment.

3. *Emotional*—Sometimes due to emotional setbacks students suffer from maladjustments, it could be sometimes due to loss of close family members, accidents or due to hormonal imbalances.

Factors of Maladjustment

1. *Physical*—weakness, illness, etc.
2. *Poverty*—inferiority complex
3. Broken home
4. Biased behaviour of parents, teachers
5. *Emotional distress*—death of loved ones, accidents, etc.

Defense Mechanisms

Repression—It is an unconscious mechanism employed by the ego to keep disturbing or threatening thoughts from becoming conscious. For example, during Oedipus complex aggression and thoughts towards same sex parents is basically a repressed behaviour of child.

Denial involves blocking external events from awareness. When a situation is difficult to handle, person's refusal to experience it or face it is considered as denial. For example, smokers generally refuse to except that smoking is injurious to health.

Projection includes individual attributing, their own unacceptable thoughts, ideas, motives and feelings to another person. For example, you might hate somebody but your superego says that this might be unacceptable and in this case individual solves the problem believing that they hate you.

Displacement—Satisfying an impulse or aggression with a substitute objects. For example, generally a man displaces the office related tensions on his family members or kicks the dog at home to displace his frustration.

Regression—This is a movement back in psychological time when one is faced with stress. For example, generally after birth of second baby elder child starts bedwetting or sucking his thumb to gain attention of their parents.

Sublimation—When an individual satisfies his impulse like aggression with a substitute object, in a socially acceptable way. For example, Sports could be a way to put our emotions or aggressions in some constructive way.

Rationalization—It is basically giving excuses to overshadow ones weaknesses. For example, a fox generally says grapes are sour when they are out of reach. Similarly, students when not have achieved well in examinations generally find faults with examination system.

Individual uses a number of methods and procedures to defend and escape from conflicts, frustration and depression, in order to better adjust in society, they are also known as defense adjustment mechanism.

1. *Overcoming blocks*—Through these mechanisms, the individual puts away the impediments that are there in the way of his success in future. If these blocks are not removed, he will not be able to do efforts in future.

2. *Reaching goals*—This mechanism helps the individual to reach the ultimate goal of his life, i.e. mental balance, through occupational adaptation is done here.

3. *Satisfying motives*—Frustration which is caused by failure or deprivation is reduced to minimum by adopting these methods. They work as alternate source of satisfying motives.

4. *Relieving tensions*—This mechanism helps in bringing the individual into another world which is full of pleasure and thus his tension is released.

5. *Maintaining equilibrium*—Maladjustment imbalances the mind for a limited period of time. This mind is again brought to the equilibrium point through this mechanism.

Bibliography

Aggarwal, J.C. (1989). *Educational Vocational Guidance and Counselling*, Delhi: Doaba House Delhi.

Agrawal, Rashmi (2017). *Educational Vocational Guidance and Counselling,* Delhi: Shipra Publications.

Anastasi, (1959). *Psychological Testing*, New York: Macmillan Co.

Bhargava, Mahesh (2003). *Manovagyanik Parikshan evam Maapan*, Agra: H.P. Bhargava Book House.

Bhatnagar, A.B. (2009). *Advanced Educational Psychology*, Meerut: International Publishing.

Crow, L.D. and Crow, A. (1962). *An Introduction to Guidance*, New Delhi: Eurasia Publicity House.

Fellham, C. and Horton, I. (2000). *Handbook of Counselling and Psychotherapy*, New York: McGraw Hills.

Jones, A.J. (1970). *Principles of Guidance*, (Indian Ed.) Bombay: Tata Mc Grow Hills Publishing Company Ltd.

Kapoor, M. (2001). Mental Health Illness and Therapy, In: Pandey, J. (ed.) *Psychology of India Revisited*, New Delhi.: Sage Publication.

Kapoor, M. (2001). *Mental Health of Indian Children*, New Delhi, Sage Publication.

Kochhar, K. (2005). *Guidance and Counseling in College and Universities*, New Delhi: Sterling Publisher Pvt. Limited.

Mathewson, R.H. (1955). *Guidance Policy and Practice*. New York: Harper and Row.

Mathur, S.S. (1985). *Clinical Psychology,* Agra: Vinod Pustak Mandir.

Miller, C.H. (1981). *Foundation of Guidance,* New York: Harper and Brothers.

Murphy, G. (1970). *An Introduction to Counselling in Schools,* New York: Harper and Row.

Nair, K.V. (1949). *Psychological Bases of Vocational Guidance*, Delhi: Meenakshi Prakashan.

Pandey, K.P. (1987). *Shakshik Vayvasayik Nirdeshan ke Aadhar*, Delhi: Amithabh Prakashan.

Pandey, K.P. (2005). *Educational and Vocational Guidance in India*, Varanasi: Vishvavidhalaya Prakashan.

Patterson, C.H. (1973). *Theories of Counselling and Psychotherapy*, New York: Harper and Row.

Ranganathan, Namita (2012). *Education for Mental Health: Rethinking Issues in Guidance and Counselling*, Delhi: Shipra Publications.

Rao, S. Narayana (1982). *Counselling Psychology*. New Delhi: Tata McGraw Hill Publishing Co. Ltd.

Ray, A. and Asthana, M. (2006). *Guidance and Counselling Concepts, Areas and Approches*, Banaras: Motilal Banarasidas Publishing Company.

Robinson, F.P. (1950). *Principles and Practices in Student Counsellling*, New York.

Roe, A. (1956). *The Psychology of Occupation*, New York: Wiley.

Roeber and Smith, C.E. Ericson (1955). *Organisation and Administration of Guidance Services*, New York: McGraw Hills.

Rogers, C.R. (1931). *Client Centered Therapy,* Boston: Houghton Maffin Co.

Saxena, Radha Rani (2009). *Guidance and Counseling in Education*, Rajasthan Hindi Granth Academy, Rawat Printers and Stationers, Jaipur.

Sharma, R.A. (2003). *Fundamentals of Guidance and Counselling*, Meerut: R. Lal Book Depots.

Smith, G.E. (1951). *Principles and Practices of the Guidance Programme*, New York.

Strang, R. (1947). *Educational Guidance: Its Principles and Practice*, New York: The Macmillan Company.

Verma, S.K. (1980). *Mental Illness and Treatment*, Sage Publications.

Walia, J.S. (2008). *Foundations of Guidance*, Jalandhar, Punjab: Ahim Paul Publisher.